Albert J. King, Homer A. King

The New Bee-Keepers' Text-Book

Volume 1

Albert J. King, Homer A. King

The New Bee-Keepers' Text-Book
Volume 1

ISBN/EAN: 9783337144647

Printed in Europe, USA, Canada, Australia, Japan

Cover: Foto ©Andreas Hilbeck / pixelio.de

More available books at **www.hansebooks.com**

THE NEW
BEE-KEEPERS' TEXT BOOK,

BY

A. J. KING,

EDITOR OF "THE BEE-KEEPERS' MAGAZINE."

TWENTY - FOURTH EDITION, FIFTY - SECOND THOUSAND.

Being a thorough revision of the Old Text Book

By N. H & H. A. KING.

ENLARGED AND ILLUSTRATED.

NEW YORK:

ORANGE JUDD COMPANY,

245 BROADWAY.

1879.

TO

BEE-KEEPERS EVERYWHERE

WHOSE CHOSEN PURSUIT HE WOULD GLADLY RENDER STILL

MORE ATTRACTIVE, PLEASANT, AND PROFITABLE,

THIS WORK IS PRESENTED

BY THE AUTHOR.

PREFACE.

The successful cultivation of the honey bee, depends upon a correct knowledge of the laws by which the economy of the hive is regulated; comply with these laws and you reap a golden harvest—disregard them and disappointment and loss are the certain result.

The following pages are designed to impart:

1st. A knowledge of these laws.

2d. Instruction how to comply with their requirements.

3d. Caution against their violation.

To accomplish these ends we have endeavored:

1st. To bring the language within the comprehension of the man of limited education and means, to whom bee-keeping commends itself on account of its large pecuniary returns for the capital and attention required.

2d. To present the practical part of the subject fully and yet briefly, believing, as we do, that condensation, to the greatest possible extent consistent with a full exposition of the subject, not only diminishes the cost but increases the value of a work of this kind.

3d. To convey the most valuable knowledge, we have drawn from every available source, not having been ambitious to write a work purely original. Yet, as theories are worthless unless founded in truth, we have only accepted facts which have been demonstrated by eminent apiarians, and confirmed by many years' experience of our own, devoted almost exclusively to bee culture.

In our investigations in apiarian science, we have received material aid from the writings of Huber, Bevan, Dzierzon, Quinby, Harbison, Langstroth, Miner, Metcalf, Wagner, and many others, both ancient and modern.

Although the demand which called this work into existence was created by the favor with which the bee-keeping public received the American side-opening hive, yet we have endeavored to adapt the instruction to the use of both common and movable-comb hives.

N. H. & H. A. KING.

PREFACE TO THE REVISED EDITION.

The size, cost, and character of the "Bee-Keepers' Text Book" procured for it a great circulation. Simplicity of language, clearness of statement, and practical directness made it for years acceptable to to the general reader and a real hand book to the apiarian. When written it was abreast of the times; but new discoveries and inventions in apiculture render it necessary to revise the book so as to furnish all needed information to thousands now entering upon this promising industry.

The old book was written in the era of patents and partly, in the interest of the American Hive, and treated partly of management in common box hives. Patents on important parts of hives are now ended, and information for management in common box hives is not now necessary.

Many good movable comb hives are made at present and the only need now is for a text book to guide the beekeeper in the various manipulations of the apiary and adapted to all the improvements in beekeeping, which is destined to become one of the great industries of America. Since the publication of the old book the invention of the Honey Extractor, and the successful use of artificial Comb-foundation have materially changed the mode of management necessary to secure the greatest results. In addition to these two great discoveries, improved smokers, feeders, and modes of securing and packing honey in boxes, jars, and packages best suited to the market, are of such importance that we now issue

THE NEW BEE-KEEPERS' TEXT BOOK,

in which all that is good in the old book is retained; that which has been out-grown, left out; and additions made, covering the full use of all improvements in bee-keeping so as to secure the very best results.

We confidently commend the "New Bee-keepers' Text Book" to all lovers of nature and all interested in this industry.

The beginner will find in it just such information and guidance as he daily needs, and the advanced apiarian will find it a useful hand-book and companion.

NEW YORK, JUNE 20TH, 1878.

INTRODUCTION.

BEE-KEEPING.

The culture of the honey bee has engaged the attention of intelligent and enterprising men of all ages; yet within a few years, by the introduction of improved movable frames and other improvements, this pursuit, always attractive, is rendered no longer a business of "luck" or chance, but as certain and more remunerative, with small capital, than any other rural occupation.

About five years ago, it was estimated, in the "American Bee Journal," that there were then seventy thousand bee-keepers in the United States, many attending to several apiaries, with from one hundred to three hundred swarms in each, and yet, with the increasing light and interest, hundreds, all over the country, are engaging in this branch of industry. In the mind of the uninformed but enquiring reader, a few questions will arise, which we will here only briefly notice, as he can refer, from the index, to each subject—more fully treated under its appropriate head.

Is there not danger of overstocking the country?

Says M. Quinby, one of the most extensive bee-keepers in the world, "this interest in bees should be encouraged to continue till enough are kept to collect all the honey now wasted, which, compared with the present collections, would be more than a thousand pounds to one."

Do not some fail of success in bee-keeping?

Yes, just as the farmer fails who neglects his fences, plows his lands when too wet, or crops them until their fertility is exhausted. So in bee-keeping. Some fail through gross neglect, or allow their bees to become so weakened by overswarming as to fall an easy prey to the moth; while others "divide" till they are left without "quotient" or "remainder." Let us profit by their experience, and prosperity will be the result.

Is not watching for swarms, hiving, &c., perplexing in large apiaries?

Yes: and you will find a complete remedy in the chapter on "Nucleus Swarming," which enables you to swarm many stocks at one time, securing to each new swarm a fertile queen, without removing the old queen from the parent stock or scarcely interrupting its labors. By this method, you will obtain a steady increase of stocks, avoid queenless swarms by loss of young queens; thus, all colonies *are kept strong*, enabling them to bid defiance to the moth-miller and other enemies. This, in the words of an eminently practical bee-keeper, "is both sure and economical;" doing away with all watching and loss by flight to the woods.

Is it true that there are only a few who understand the secret of handling or "charming" bees?

That there are a few who claim to have some great secret, and convince gaping crowds by performing tricks and wonderful [?] feats with bees, (not forgetting to pocket the proceeds of the supposed secret,) we readily admit. Yet, it is also true that there are hundreds of successful bee-keepers in the United States, who esteem the good of the cause and their reputation, of more value than money thus obtained from the uninformed, and freely communicate instruction how to safely perform all needful operations. One of them says, "acquaint yourself with the *principles of management,* * * and you will find that you have little more reason to dread the sting of a bee than the horns of a favorite cow, or the heels of your faithful horse."

WHO SHOULD KEEP BEES?

We reply, all classes who want a healthy, pleasant and profitable occupation.

Says Rev. Robert Baird, "there are few portions of our country which are not admirably adapted to the culture of the honey bee. The wealth of the nation might be increased by millions of dollars, if every family favorably situated, would keep a few hives. No other branch of industry can be named, in which there need be so little loss on the material employed, or which so completely derives its profits from the vast and exhaustless domains of nature."

The Farmer should keep Bees to collect the honey afforded by his orchards, timber lands and broad pasture fields; for "profit must attend success in this branch of the farmer's stock, inasmuch as bees work for nothing and find themselves."

The Mechanic should keep Bees, as those who work in wood can make their own hives, beside supplying their neighbors; and all will find that, for the little time and capital required, it will materially affect their expenses and income.

The Horticulturist should keep Bees to gather the delicious nectar which "would else be lost on desert air," and also to mingle the pollen of flowers, for

> Trees will flourish all the more,
> When flowers mate by rifled store.

The Invalid, by spending a portion of his time in the open air, caring for his bees, will not only find his purse replenished, but, what is better, returning health.

> He who with health would live at ease,
> Should cultivate both fruit and bees;
> Much labor though the first demands,
> The second 's for more feeble hands.

The Merchant and Professional Man, and all who spend much of their time *indoors*, will find in bee-keeping a pleasant, healthful outdoor pastime, invigorating to both mind and body.

Those who own no land may keep Bees. In raising horses or cattle, one must own or hire his pasture lands. They are very serviceable, but they *must be fed*. Bees require but little room, and find their own food; for "roam where they will, the whole region is their common."

The Aged, and in short, *every person*, who wishes to engage in a light occupation, which will secure health, ease and independence, should give this subject an earnest and candid examination

Bees multiply rapidly, and one who has ten stocks, may, with care, soon expect to have a hundred, and a moderate increase need not interfere with a large annual harvest of honey.

To the wants of what class of mankind has not the Creator admirably adapted the industry of this insect, and how eloquently this adaptation speaks of his goodness, wisdom and care for the welfare of his creatures?

TABLE OF CONTENTS.

	PAGE.
COPIOUS ALPHABETICAL INDEX	13
CHAPTER I. Physiology of Bees	19
CHAPTER II. Natural Swarming	25
CHAPTER III. Bee Pasturage and Products	45
CHAPTER IV. Extractors, Comb Foundations, Surplus Honey in Boxes and Extracted, Marketing Honey	58
CHAPTER V. Artificial Swarming	94
CHAPTER VI. The Apiary	124
CHAPTER VII. Diary of Honey Plants	160
CHAPTER VIII. Monthly Management	181
CHAPTER IX. Hives	200
CHAPTER X. Biography of Bee Keepers	212

ALPHABETICAL INDEX.

Absconding Swarms, 26, 27—How Prevented, 32—How Captured ... 128
Advantages of Bee Keeping, 9—Who should Keep Bees, 11—Profits of, 74 ... 157
Advantages of the Nucleus System of Swarming ... 105
Advantages Secured in the Construction of Hives ... 201
After Swarming, 33—Cause of and How Prevented ... 34
Age of Bees, 20—Queens, 20—Drones, 21—Worker ... 22
Alsike Clover ... 168
Apiary, 124—Best Location, 125—How to Stock it, 127—Monthly Management .. 181
Anger of Bees, 10—How Subdued ... 42
Ants, How to Banish them from the Apiary ... 143
Artificial Swarming—Time for, 95—Different Methods ... 97
August Management ... 194
Bar Hives and Bar Frames used in Germany ... 202
Basswood or Linden affords much Choice Honey ... 46, 51, 163
Bee Bread or Pollen, 51—Rye Meal Best Substitute for ... 52
Bee Feeders ... 155
Bee Glue or Propolis ... 52
Bee Houses, 126—A Shed Best and how Constructed ... 126
Bee Keeping, 9—Profits of, 157—How to Commence ... 128
Bee Pasturage, 45—Crops Most Valuable for both Seed and Honey ... 49
Bee Stings, 79—How to Neutralize the Poison ... 44

ALPHABETICAL INDEX.

Bee's Tongue 78
Bee Veil...44, 84
Bees, Three Classes, 19—Worker, 22—Queen, 21—Her Fertilization, 32—Her
    Loss, 35—Signs of 56
Bees, Killing with Brimstone to Obtain Honey.. 201
Bees, Natural Swarming, 25—Hiving, 21—How to Prevent them from Leaving
    the Hive, 32—Wintering.. 146
Bees Wild, How to Hunt Them, 130—How to Trap Robbers or Wild Bees
    Without Finding the Tree 133
Bees, Italian, 107—Superiority of, 109—How to Change Stocks of Common
    Black Bees to Italians... 114
Bees, Monthly Managent of, 181—Quieting and Handling, 42—Moving, 135
    —Transferring Bees and Combs into Frame Hives.................................136, 138
Beeswax Extractor...60, 89
Bellows Smoker.. 43
Borage 175
Boneset or Thoroughwort... 176
Biography of Bee Keepers...212, 229
Boxes for Surplus Honey, 63—How to Induce the Bees to Commence and
    Continue Working in them.. 66
Breeding... 23
Buckwheat a Valuable Pasturage, 47—Time of Sowing..................................... 50
Buying Bees, How to Select Valuable Stock... 127
Cage for Queen,..122
Candy as Food for Bees in Winter,...153
Catnip as a Honey Crop...46—51
Catnip, Motherwort and Hoarhound,..175
Caution to the Beginner,.. 84
Cells, different size of Drone and Worker, 24—Royal Cells.............................102
Cocoon spun by Young Bee as left in the Cell,... 56
Colony, if Prosperous, consists of,... 19
Color of Hives,... 205
Comb Foundation, 61—How to Fasten in Frame, 87—Advantage of Using it,......88
Comb, Composition of, 52—To secure it Built True in Frames,........................ 54
Comb, Drone and Worker, 24, 100—To Preserve from Moth,..........................144
Comb, only Defective to be Removed, 56—Melting into Wax........................... 57
City Bee Keeping,... 71
Consumption of Honey,... 74
Cultivating Honey Crops,... 49
Dampness Injurious to Bees,..56, 151
December Management,.. 198
Defective Combs,... 56
Dedication,... 3
Deformed Cells,... 77

ALPHABETICAL INDEX.

Derivation of word Bee,..76
Description of New Improvements,...86
Diary of Honey Plants,..160, 180
Dividing,...97
Doubling Stocks Yearly by Nucleus Swarming,......................................106
Driving or Forced Swarming,...97
Drones, 21—Drone Comb, 24, 100—Drone Cells,..................................77
Eggs, Number Laid, 20—How Fecundated, 21—Time to Mature,.......24
February Management,...182
Feeding Bees,...153
Fertility of Queen, 20—Decreases with Age, 37—Italian most Prolific,....109
Fertilization of Young Queens,...82
Fertilization in Confinement,..210
Flowers for Bees,..46
Flour a Substitute for Pollen,..52
Foul Brood,..209
Frames, Moveable, their Invention and Improvement,.......................202
Fruit Trees,...160
Fruit Tree Flowers Valuable to Induce Early Swarming,..................24, 45
Golden Rod and Asters,...171, 175
Handling Bees,...42
Hatching and Fertilization of Queens,...32
Hives, 200—Hive Essentials,..203
Honey Boxes,...63
Honey Comb,..77
Honey Crate,...67
Honey Crops,..49
Honey, Different Qualities Gathered, 45—Stored in Frames, 129—In Boxes,......200
Honey Extractor, 59, 60—Advantages of..91
Honey Industry,..74
How to Prevent Swarms from Leaving their Hives,............................32
How to Prevent Swarms from Clustering together,............................29
How to Separate Them,..30
How to get the Comb Built True in the Frame,...................................54
How to Stock an Apiary,..127
Hunting Wild Bees, 130—Trapping Them..133
Introduction,...9
Introducing an Italian Queen...115, 117
Increase of Stocks..15
Impregnation of Queen Bee...20, 33, 103
Importance of New Blood in the Apiary..111
Italian Honey Bee...107
Italian Queen Rearing..114, 118, 120
Italianizing a Whole Apiary...116

ALPHABETICAL INDEX.

January Management	181
June Management	190
July Management	192
Locust Tree a Great Honey Producer	46
Loss of Queens, 35—Signs of	37
Lucerne Clover	169
Making Hives in Winter	204
March Management	184
May Management	188
Marketing Honey	67
Medicinal Power of Honey	73
Melilot	170
Melting Comb into Wax	57
Mingonette	177
Moth-Miller, Fear Misdirected	142
Monthly Managment	181
Movable Comb Hive	203
Moving Bees	125
Mustard	46, 50, 178
Natural Swarming	25
Non-Swarming	41
November Management	198
Nucleus Swarming, 101—Advantages of	105
Observation Hive	206
October Managment	196
Ovaries of the Queen Bee	81
Over Stocking	47
Painting Hives	205
Perennial Plants	167
Piping of Young Queens	34
Pollen, or Bee Bread	51
Poplar or Tulip Tree Secretes much Honey	46
Preface	5
Preface to the Revised Edition	7
Prevention of Swarming	41
Profits of the Apiary	156
Propolis or Bee Glue	52
Purchasing Bees	127
Queen Bee, 19—Hatching and Fertilization of, 33—Loss of	35
Queen Cage, 122—Queen Cell, 77-80—How Transferred	102
Queenless Stocks, 35—Signs	36
Quieting Bees	42
Raspberries Yield Much Fine Honey	46, 162
Removing Honey Boxes	94

ALPHABETICAL INDEX.   xvii

Removing Defective Comb	56
Robbing, 140—Trapping Robbers or Wild Bees	133
Royal Cells, 26, 33, 162—Royal Jelly	25
Raising Italian Queens as a Business	11
Rye Meal Best Substitute for Pollen to Induce Early Breeding	52
Second and Third Swarms or After Swarms	33
September Management	195
Shipping Queens	122
Stands	124, 125
Smoke to Quiet Bees	43
Small Fruits	162
Small Boxes for the Nuclei,	119
Southern Honey Trees	163
Sour-Wood or Sorrel-Tree	165
Stings, How to Neutralize the Poison	44
Statistics of the Honey Industry	74
Surplus Honey, 105—In Boxes	89
Swarming Natural, 25—Signs of, 27—Prevention of	41
Swarming Artificial, 95—Nucleus	109
Taking Bees on Shares	128
Taking up Light Stock	129
Tansy to Banish Ants	143
The Sumac	166
Teasel	175
The Circular Saw	206
Title Page	1
Transferring Bees and Comb from Box Hives	136–138
Trees for Pasturage, 48—For Shade	125
Uncapping Knife	59
Uniting Stocks	39
Uses of Honey	68
Ventilation	147, 197
View of our Home Apiary	76
Wax	57
White Clover, 45—As a Honey Crop	49
Who Should Keep Bees	11
Wire Foundation	55
Wintering Bees	145, 152
Worker Cells	77
Worker Bee, 22—Worker Comb	24
Worms	144, 145
Wren	143

ILLUSTRATIONS.

Abdomen of Worker Bee Magnified	53
Alsike Clover	168
Bass-wood	164
Bee's Sting	79
Bee's Tongue	78
Bees-wax Extractor	60
Bellows Smoker	43
Blue Aster	174
Body of Bee	82
Brood Comb	26
Circular Saw	208
Comb Foundation Machine	62
Eggs Shown in the Cells	80
Fertile Queen	33
Golden Rod	172
Honey Comb	77
Honey Crate	67
Honey Extractor	58
Honey in Boxes and Bottles	68
Larvæ and Royal Jelly	80
Leg of Bee	82
Male and Female Moth Miller	142
Melilot	171
Oblong Munn Frame	203
Ovaries of the Queen Bee	81
Portrait of W. W. Cary	225
Portrait of Rev. Father Dzierzon	227
Portrait of Francis Huber	213
Portrait of Rev. H. A. King	220
Portrait of Prof. Leuckart	224
Portrait of Rev. L. L. Langstroth	218
Portrait of Moses Quinby	216
Portrait of Rev. E. Van Slyke	229
Portrait of Baron Von Berlepsch	221
Portrait of Capt. T. B. Siebold	222
Queen Cells	32
Queen Cell Cut Open	80
Queen Cell Inserted	102
Queen Drone and Worker Bee	19
Taylor's Frame	204
Transfering Tools	136
Uncapping Knife	59
View of our Home Apiary	76

CHAPTER I.

PHYSIOLOGY OF THE THREE CLASSES.

A PROSPEROUS colony of bees, at the beginning of the "swarming season," consists of a fertile queen, a few hundred drones and about forty thousand workers. The annexed cuts will give a fair representation of the three classes into which this insect community is divided.

Queen.

Drone.

Worker.

THE QUEEN is a perfectly developed female, and the prolific parent of the whole colony—the mother of every bee it contains. "Mother Bee" is her most appropriate and truthful name, as laying eggs appears to be the sole end of her existence, and the only duty she performs. This fact is beautifully demonstrated by removing a native queen and introducing an Italian queen in her stead. If the change is made in November, few common bees will remain by the following May; or if made in June, the yellow workers will begin to appear in a few weeks, and by September scarcely a black bee can be found in the hive. In the height of honey gathering, and under the most favorable circumstances the queen will deposit about three thousand eggs per day. She is distinguished from the other bees by her form, color and size, being longer and darker colored upon the back than either drone or worker. But the Italian queen is much lighter colored than either the Italian drone or worker, the larger part of her body being of a golden yellow.

The queen is of slender structure, with comparatively short wings, and is usually recognized by her measured matronly movements and her long, finely tapered abdomen.

She usually lives from three to four years. If her death occur when there are drones in the apiary and young worker brood or eggs in the hive, or if she is soon to leave the hive with a first swarm, the workers construct large cells, supplying them with "royal jelly," and the eggs or larvæ that would otherwise have produced worker bees are developed into queens. Only one queen is allowed to remain in the hive. The queen has a curved sting, but will use it only when contending with rival queens, as she cannot tolerate a rival within the hive. Eggs are sometimes laid by the young queen before her impregnation, but they invariably produce drones. She usually leaves the hive when about five days old to meet the drones in the air for impregnation, which—once accomplished—suffices for life, as ordinarily she never afterwards leaves the hive except when accompanying a first swarm. The drone semen or sperm is retained in the spermatheca of the queen, a small sac near the point of her abdomen, and when laying, as the egg passes from the queen's ovary, it is brought in contact with the drone sperm to produce workers, or is allowed to pass without such contact to produce drones, the same as eggs laid before her impregnation. Some have supposed this contact to be produced by compression of the queen's abdomen, caused by the size of the cells in which workers are reared, they being much smaller than drone cells. This theory is disproved by the fact that a stock deprived of its drone-comb, will sometimes rear drones in worker cells; besides, in comb-building, the queen will frequently deposit eggs in the cells while their walls are scarcely an eighth of an inch long and could cause no pressure.

THE DRONE.

"The drones are the males, and do not work for the support of the hive, but lead an idle life, feeding upon the produce of others' labor."—RICHARDSON.

The drones are more bulky, though somewhat shorter, than the queen, and, unlike her, their wings are long enough to cover the entire abdomen. They are much larger than the workers, and have a clumsy, uncouth appearance. When flying, their loud, boisterous hum is easily recognized. Being without a sac for carrying honey or grooves on their thighs for pollen, they are physically disqualified for performing any labors of the hive. Their proboscis is too short for extracting the nectar from flowers, and being destitute of a sting, they cannot assist in protecting the stores from robbery. They are called into existence at the approach of the swarming season to fertilize the young queens. As impregnation is effected while on the wing, the drones leave the hive in considerable numbers about noon, on fine days, and the young queens make their excursions soon after. Whenever this service is supposed to be accomplished for the season, they are relentlessly driven forth and destroyed by the workers. A stock of bees that has lost its queen and failed to rear another, will retain drones after all others are destroyed, and frequently throughout the winter. Without drones the young queens would remain barren, and the race soon become extinct. The number of drones in a hive is often very large, amounting to hundreds and even thousands. In a state of nature, or where but one or two hives are kept, a greater proportion of drones are necessary as the young queen, when making her "bridal trip," should be sure of a speedy meeting, for, when roaming long in search of one, she is more liable to accidents. Where several colonies are kept, if each rear a few dozen drones there will be enough, in the aggregate, for all practical purposes. In movable comb hives all excess of drone comb should be removed, and the production of useless consumers thus prevented.

THE WORKER.

The workers, although the most diminutive in size of the three classes, are alike the wonder and admiration of the student of nature.

When we consider their *unvarying* God implanted instincts, whether displayed in hoarding rich stores for future use, in their matchless architectural skill, as seen in comb-building, or in their entire devotion to the welfare of the queen and her numerous, maturing progeny, we are constrained to regard them as the most wonderful class of this insect family. The average age of the worker is but a few weeks during summer, and from six to nine months during the cooler part of the year.

As regards the sex of the workers, modern writers agree in classing them as undeveloped females. They are incapable of fertilization by the drone, yet, occasionally in queenless colonies, one will be found laying eggs, which, being unfertilized, never produce workers but drones only.

This laying need not be mistaken as the work of a fertile queen, for, unlike her uniform laying, these eggs are deposited regardless of order, some cells containing several and others none. The bees destroy the excess, and the remaining eggs produce perfect drones.

The workers are so well known that a minute description would seem superfluous in a Hand Book. Upon them devolves all the labor of collecting and defending the stores, building comb, feeding and protecting the queen and brood, and expelling the drones when they are no longer necessary to the well-being of the colony. In short, they rule and regulate the whole economy of the hive, performing all its offices except those which have direct reference to the reproduction of the species.

BREEDING.

The yield of honey strength of the colony, the season of the year, and other circumstances have considerable influence, both on the amount of brood reared and the time required for its development. In this latitude, the average time from the laying of the egg to the appearance of the perfect insect, is, for the worker, twenty-one days; for the drone, twenty-four; and for the queen, about sixteen days. The cells, in which the workers are reared, are the smallest in size, those for drones nearly one-third larger, and a queen cell still larger and of peculiar form, requiring as much material for its construction as fifty worker cells. In strong colonies, having plenty of stores, the queen will often deposit eggs in every month of the year, the least brood being reared between October and January. During this time the brood often occupies a small circle in the centre of the cluster of bees exactly opposite on each side of a comb. Smaller circles are next occupied in the two adjoining combs. The circle of eggs in the first comb is then enlarged, and more added in the others, continuing to spread to other combs, keeping the distance from the centre or place of beginning to the outside of the circle about equal on all sides. The effect of this is to produce a concentration and economy of the animal heat for developing the various changes of the brood. On the approach of spring, an increased amount of brood is reared, and as early spring flowers appear the bees go to work in earnest, to provide limpid honey and freshly gathered pollen for the queen and her numerous offspring. When the fruit trees unfold their pink and snowy blossoms, rich supplies are garnered by the busy throng of workers. Breeding goes on apace. The latent swarming impulse begins to be felt, and if the weather continues warm and balmy, we soon arrive at the swarming season.

CHAPTER II.

NATURAL SWARMING.

The swarming season is one of unusual interest to the bee-keeper. He hopes soon to commence his annual harvest both of swarms and surplus honey. The issue of natural swarms is almost wholly dependent upon continued warm growing weather. June is the great swarming month in the northern States. Yet, when the spring is unusually favorable, we get an occasional swarm as early as the middle of May, and many about the last of that month. Again, swarming may not commence until July. Bees will often rear drones, construct queen cells, and be just on the point of swarming, when a few days of bad weather will cause the drones and embryo queens to be destroyed, and swarming to be postponed indefinitely. As much time must be spent in preparation when this occurs, it will require several weeks before swarms can issue, though the weather be never so favorable.

Bees, like some human beings, seem most discontented when most prosperous. If the season is favorable, the May flowers will scarcely have appeared till the swarming fever begins instinctively to steal over the colony, affecting equally, perhaps, both queen and workers. The first step of preparation taken is the rearing of drones, by an early deposit of eggs in the drone cells by the queen. As these mature and the "lusty fellows"

NATURAL SWARMING.

throng the entrance, if the weather is warm and pasturage abundant, a few queen cells will be commenced at different times by the workers. These, in most cases, are suspended from the edges or inequalities of the combs, with their open end downward. From three to ten queen cells are commonly constructed, and the egg or larvæ, is lavishly supplied with "royal jelly," a pungent, stimulating, light cream-colored substance, when the cell is further lengthened down and sealed over. It is now about an inch long, and resembles a pea-nut in shape and appearance. In movable comb hives, these queen cells are easily found by looking over the combs about the time swarms are expected. You can hardly mistake them even though you never saw one before. It is better to swarm bees artificially and not wait for natural swarming. But since bees (will) sometimes swarm when carefully managed, and since beekeepers are sometimes unable for some reason to give attention before they swarm, all should understand the indications of swarming and the modes of hiving swarms. Bees are not apt to swarm before the hive is strong in numbers, young bees are hatching in abundance, drones are flying, and the weather is pleasant. These are not, however, sure indications of swarming.

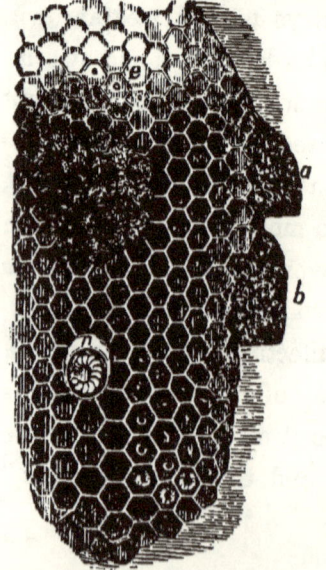

4. This cut represents brood in various stages from eggs and larvæ in the lower part of the comb to brood capped at x, and just emerging at f; x, is a queen cell just commenced from larvæ; b, a perfect queen cell capped over; a, a cell from which the queen has just emerged.

The progress of these cells is the only certain indication of swarming, and when one or more have been capped over, the swarm is ready to leave for its new and sometimes distant home. The first warm, clear day is generally improved, when the mass of workers, after hastily filling their sacs with provisions for their journey, rush "pell mell" from the hive, accompanied by the queen, with great "noise and confusion."

After flying a short time, they usually cluster upon some overhanging branch, more or less elevated. Hives should be kept in readiness, as success depends greatly upon promptness in hiving swarms as they issue, for, if left hanging in the heat of the sun, they soon become impatient and often fly off and are lost in consequence.

HIVING BEES.

The process of hiving is extremely simple and pretty generally understood; if the new hive is *cool* and *clean* the bees are not slow in taking possession. If the swarm has clustered upon a bush or tree near the ground, spread down a sheet or piece of canvas directly under or as near the swarm as practicable. If a table will bring the hive very near the cluster use one. Remove the cover and quilt and shake the bees directly into the hive if convenient. If not, jar the bees in front of the hive after opening the front entrances, or raising the hive an inch from the bottom board, leaving no opening beneath, which they may mistake for the hive, and guide them to the entrance with a twig. Some will soon discover the new home, and by their joyful hum communicate the glad tidings to the whole swarm. Having filled themselves with honey before leaving the old hive, they are usually peaceable and almost as harmless as flies. If they should clog the entrance, disturb them gently with the feather end of a quill, and, if any cluster upon the outside, brush them down and see that all enter lest the queen be left out. Now, let the hive down upon the board, and immediately carry it to the place it is intended to occupy in the apiary. Raise the front edge half an inch, and *shade the hive from the sun.* The few bees left flying will soon return to the old stock from which the swarm issued. But if the swarm is left where it was hived till evening, many bees will have commenced gathering honey, and, having carefully marked their new location, will, as they fly out, the next morning return to this place and perish. If a swarm should cluster upon a high limb or body of a tree, ascend upon a ladder and shake or brush them into a basket, and cover it over with a cloth to prevent their flying. The basket may be lowered with a cord to an assistant, or brought down, and gently poured upon the sheet at the entrance of the hive. When the swarm has clustered upon a small limb, it may be carefully severed without disturbing the cluster, and carried to the hive. Hold them to the entrance until some discover the hive, when all will gladly enter.

If a swarm cluster in some inaccessible place, as the forks of a tree, they may often be induced to enter a box inverted above them, by smoking or slightly sprinkling them with water, or by partly covering the box to make it resemble the entrance to a hive, brush a few in and they will soon call in the whole swarm. From the box they are shaken directly into the hive, or made to enter from the raised front as before. A hiving basket is easily made by taking a small basket and covering one side of the top with cloth. To the handle and the rim of the covered side of the basket a handle is fixed which may be lengthened by fixing to it pieces of different lengths. This is raised directly under the swarm and the bees jarred from the limb into it and then poured into the hive. In this way hiving is quickly accomplished; and dispatch in hiving is important, as in very large apiaries, if natural swarming is permitted, much difficulty is often experienced from two or more swarms issuing about the same time, when, unless prevented, they are almost certain to unite. It is some trouble to separate them and have a queen for each. Therefore, when many swarms are expected, the apiary should be closely watched.

TO GUARD AGAINST SWARMS CLUSTERING TOGETHER.

At times, the swarming fever seems to be contagious. One swarm will scarcely have settled till another stock, and another, will send forth their crazy legions to darken the air and make "confusion worse confounded." The watchful bee-keeper will judge from the state of the weather and the condition of his stocks, when these things are likely to happen. While a swarm is issuing, if other colonies "hang out" threateningly, he should immediately sprinkle these outsiders with water, or blow a few whiffs of smoke into each hive. This will slightly disconcert them, and probably give time for hiving the swarm already out. If, however, one should start when the first is but partially hived, let him quickly cover it with a sheet to prevent a union, and give his attention to the new comers. These must now be hived; and when mostly in, if no others have started, uncover the first, that the stragglers flying may be divided between the two. But, should the second swarm start before the first has settled, he will hardly prevent their clustering together. After a swarm has started it is impossible to check it, without closing the entrance, which would be a dangerous and often fatal experiment. Beside, the queen may have been among the first to start, and she would be a serious loss.

When two swarms unite, if the bee-keeper's time is precious and his hive large enough, he may hive them together. When put in the movable comb hive, give such double swarms access to the surplus boxes immediately. They will usually store about one-third more surplus honey than a single swarm, but they will be worth no more at the end of the season, than each would have been had they remained separate. Hence, if the swarms are early and large, and the weather continues favorable, it is better to divide the swarm at the end of a week. (See "Nucleus Swarming.") However, if a movable-comb hive is not at hand, it will pay to take some trouble

TO SEPARATE SWARMS THAT CLUSTER TOGETHER.

In separating two swarms that have clustered together, the object is to get a queen for each. To do this, spread down a sheet, placing an empty hive upon each end. Shake your bees upon the sheet between the hives and sprinkle them with a little water, which will retard their movements and give a good chance to see the queens as they pass along. With a quill or brush, start the bees each way, having two or three feet for them to travel to reach each hive. Keep the bees moving and the entrances open. Watch for the queen near one entrance, while an assistant watches at the other hive. Both queens are often seen as they crawl over the sheet. If both are found, divide the bees equally, giving a queen to each hive, and the work is done. Should you find but one, secure her in a tumbler. Divide the bees about equally, and, by watching them a few minutes, you will soon see where your queen is needed, as those without a queen will show the usual symptoms, by running about the entrance and up the outside of the hive as if in search of something. Present the queen to them and they will soon become quiet. But, should neither queen be seen, you stand one chance in two of getting a queen in each hive. Watch them fifteen or twenty minutes. If one shows signs of being queenless close up the entrances and remove to the stand it is to occupy, being careful to give sufficient ventilation. Now, shake the part that has the queens again upon the sheet, making them travel some distance to reach the hive. You will seldom fail to find one of the queens. Secure her in a tumbler or queen cage, and as soon as all the bees are in, remove the hive to its permanent stand. Open the other hive and place the queen at the entrance and the bees will receive her joyfully. The two hives should be placed some distance apart on separate stands, and each should have a comb or two of brood inserted.

TO PREVENT NEW SWARMS FROM LEAVING THEIR HIVES.

Natural swarms will occasionally refuse to stay after having been hived, usually in consequence of heat or strong odors about the hive. In nucleus swarming this seldom or never happens, because the bees are never without a comb containing brood and honey; and this they will not leave voluntarily. Therefore, when hiving a swarm in a movable-comb hive, go to any stock that can spare a comb containing brood and honey. Brush back the bees, being careful not to remove the queen or any queen-cells with the comb, and place it in the hive that is to receive the new swarm. It will not only prevent the bees from decamping but will greatly encourage them, and should bad weather confine them to the hive they will be secure from starvation. If the swarm is put in a common hive, place over them a box of honey, taken from the parent stock.

HATCHING AND FERTILIZATION OF QUEENS

Queen cells destroyed.

In about eight days after the old queen leaves with the first swarm, the most advanced sealed queen is ready to emerge. During this time the old stock is without a hatched queen. The young queen immediately upon leaving her cell, if not restrained by the workers, commences the work of destruction upon her yet imprisoned sisters. She accomplishes this by biting open the side of each cell near its base, and dispatching the unfortunate inmate with her sting. She is yet incompetent for the maternal duty, and must leave the hive to meet the drones in the air for

HATCHING AND FERTILIZATION OF QUEENS. 33

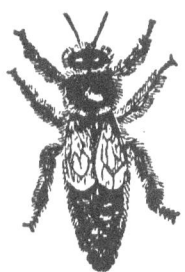

Fertile Queen.

the purpose of fertilization. This once accomplished, the workers, awaiting her safe return, greet her with a reverence and affection never shown before. They hasten to prepare the cells to receive her tiny eggs, and seem to realize that on her the existence and perpetuation of the family depends. There is also a perceptible change in the queen's form, her abdomen being a little swollen and somewhat lengthened, but not as much as at the height of the breeding season. She now remains the fruitful mother of the prosperous and happy colony.

Unimpregnated Queen.

SECOND AND THIRD OR AFTER SWARMS.

After the first swarm leaves the hive, if bees are still numerous and the yield of honey continues good, the workers will often decide to protect the queen cells, and thus cause the issue of one or more after-swarms. Small knots of bees cluster about the cells, and thus prevent their destruction by the first emerging queen. At this she seems greatly enraged and utters a peculiar sound, like the "peep," "peep," of young chickens, though on a very fine key. This is often answered in a hoarser note, from the eldest of the still enclosed queens. The senior queen continues "piping," as it is called for a day or two, meanwhile making every effort to engage in "mortal combat" her royal rivals. Being frustrated in every attempt, she finally leaves the hive in a "huff," accompanied by a considerable body of workers. It appears from this that the *immediate* cause of after-swarming springs from a desire to avoid a quarrel among the "women folks." The piping cannot be mistaken for any other sound given by the bees, and may always be heard the morning or evening preceding the issue of any swarm after the first. If a second swarm is to issue, piping will usually be heard, by holding the ear close to the hive, on the morning or evening of the eighth or ninth day from the departure of the first swarm; and, for third swarms, on the next evening or morning after the issue of the second. If it is not heard by the fourteenth day, from the time the first swarm left, no after-swarm need be expected. In good seasons or in favored localities, second swarms, if early, will generally lay up sufficient stores for winter, and are valuable on account of having vigorous young queens. But, in this latitude, if after-swarms are cast the old stock is often greatly weakened, and consequently more exposed to the inroads of the moth, besides seldom storing surplus honey after swarming. The swarms also often fail to secure stores for winter, and have to be broken up in the fall. A safer and more profitable course is to allow but one swarm to issue from a stock the same season. With movable-comb hives, the issue of after-swarms is easily and surely prevented, by opening the hive in five or six days after the first swarm leaves and taking away all the queen cells but one. By this course, we may keep all our stocks, both old and new, strong and prosperous. We give directions concerning afterswarms because from sickness, or otherwise, the beekeeper may be unable to give attention before they issue. All swarms after the second should

SECOND AND THIRD OR AFTER SWARMS.

after taking away their queens, be returned to the stocks whence they issued.

As third swarms are usually attended by several queens, it saves trouble to hive the swarm and let it stand by the old stock until the next morning, when all but one of the queens will be killed and the remaining queen may be found by jarring the bees on a sheet.

When after-swarms are expected, the apiary must be closely watched. First swarms seldom issue earlier than nine o'clock or later than three, and usually choose a fine clear day. Not so with after swarms. They are liable to issue at almost any time during the day, and often in cloudy weather. They are apt to go farther from the hive to cluster than first swarms, and, being very small, are not always found unless seen while upon the wing. Second swarms ordinarily issue in from eight to twelve days from the first; and all after-swarms must be out by the eighteenth day, after which no more swarms need be looked for from that hive, unless a "buckwheat swarm" is thrown off in August, which is an unusual occurrence.

LOSS OF QUEENS.

If a queen is lost or removed from a colony, when there are eggs or young larvæ in the worker combs and drones in the apiary, the workers almost immediately commence constructing queen cells to repair the loss. In due time a queen comes forth, and when every rival in the hive, whether mature or in embryo, has been destroyed, the remaining queen must run some risk of being lost in her flight to meet the drones for impregnation. Likewise, when a stock has swarmed, there remains in it a young queen to be fertilized. Consequently, should she be lost on her "bridal tour" the stock is left without either a queen or material from which to rear one, as the eggs left by the old queen at her departure, with the first swarm, are too far advanced to be used for that purpose.

Queens are seldom lost except while making these excursions, when they are sometimes caught by birds, but far more frequently slain as intruders by entering the wrong hive on their return, mistaking it for their own. The bereaved colony will exhibit the greatest agitation. Bees will be running about the entrance and up the sides of the hive, searching everywhere for their beloved queen. This commotion is very noticeable the next morning after the loss, while other colonies are quiet, and for two or three mornings as it gradually wears off. The bees will sometimes work with their accustomed vigor, and, still hoping to succeed in rearing another queen, their drones are preserved, after those of other stocks are destroyed. There being no farther increase in the colony, it dwindles away as daily losses occur, and, should the bee-keeper not come to the rescue, must ere long fall a prey to worms and robbers. The loss of queens is usually the result of placing hives of the same color or general appearance too close together. Colonies that have *young queens* to be impregnated should stand five feet or more apart. Such colonies are all old stocks that have cast swarms, and all swarms after the first from any stock. Also, if the hives appear much alike, each one should have a different mark to guide its queen in returning to her hive.

Unimpregnated queens should be examined about the twelfth day from the time the first swarm left, and, if no eggs are found in the combs by the eighteenth day, the stock is probably queenless. Give them a reserve *fertile* queen or queen-cell, if either is at hand. If not, take from another hive a frame of worker comb containing eggs and young brood, and place it near the centre of the queenless hive. Queens ordinarily lose their fertility or die of old age, when from three to four years old. If this happens in winter or early spring, break up the colony, before its stores tempt other stocks to robbery, giving the bees to another colony. Such a stock can seldom be induced to rear a queen at this season if furnished with material, and even though it should, the bees would nearly all be gone before she could replenish its wasting population, should she eventually chance to become fertile.

In the Spring the bee-keeper may be sure of the presence of a queen in any hive without opening it if he finds among the droppings, eggs or immature bees. It is an indication of queenlessness if the workers bring in little or no pollen when the other colonies are carrying in plump pellets upon their thighs. It is always best in early spring to open every colony so as to be sure not only of the presence of a queen but also of their general condition, and especially of the amount of stores so as to know whether it is necessary to feed, and if so to what extent. If worker eggs or brood is found, it is conclusive evidence that a fertile queen is present. But, if only the scattering oval caps are seen, join the bees to another colony, and preserve the combs for new swarms, or to exchange for frames of sealed honey.

Another method which will be found to work well if the weather is warm is to take from a stock which has an abundance of eggs and brood, one frame of brood and the queen, give them to this weak stock in exchange for a frame of empty comb; and in the heat of the day when the bees are flying the thickest exchange places with these hives. Now, put on a feeder, if honey is not plentiful in the flowers, and give them a little each day, just sufficient to keep them working and the queen will not be slow in filling all the available space with eggs, and this poor stock will soon be in a flourishing condition, while the stock from which the queen was taken will at once proceed to rear another by constructing queen cells. In ten days from the time the queen was removed, these cells will be ready to hatch, and as but one can be utilized by this stock the others may be profitably used in building up stocks in the same condition as the one just described, but in removing queen cells it is always well to leave more than one so as to be sure of a queen in case of any unforeseen occurrence. In all these operations good judgment is of the highest importance in order to discriminate between the different methods and select the one best applicable to the case in hand.

THE SAVING OF BEES.

UNITING WEAK SWARMS.

"*The greatest profit lies in saving bees, not in killing them.*"— EDWARD PRINCE.

The old practice of destroying the bees, in order to secure the honey, thus throwing away all prospect of future gain, for a little present advantage, is not only cruel but wholly unnecessary, and should be discountenanced by every admirer of this untiring little busybody.

Two weak families, when united, will consume little, if any more honey, than each would if left separate. The reason of this is, a strong colony is able to maintain the proper degree of warmth in cold weather, which greatly lessens the consumption of food. As soon as the autumn frosts have killed the flowers, colonies that are too weak to protect their stores are much exposed to robbery. Such, may either be strengthened by bringing bees from a distance, (see "How to Collect an Apiary,") or two of them may be joined together. When uniting stocks, smoke them thoroughly and shake the bees into a box or upon a sheet, together. Sprinkle them with sweetened water to prevent quarreling, and to keep them quiet, and hive as a single swarm. Stocks in the movable-comb hive may be united without shaking the bees from the combs, if early in the spring or in cool weather in the fall, or when the flowers yield a bountiful supply of honey, as the bees are then very peaceable. Treat them to tobacco smoke, which will induce all to fill themselves with honey, and serve to give them the same scent. Remove the combs with the bees adhering and place them together in the same hive, leaving out the frames containing the least honey. If one of the queens is known to be very old, she may be taken away. After closing the hive, place it upon the stand previously occupied by the stronger of the united swarms. In uniting bees, when the weather is warm enough for them to fly, it must not be forgotten that, unless carried a. mile or more away, they are strongly inclined to return to their old stand. To prevent this, give abundant ventilation, and close the entrance till near sunset. Close it again early next morning, opening it half an hour before sunset to permit the bees to fly. On the morning of the third day blow a little smoke into the hive and leave the entrance open, as the removed colony will not now return to its former stand. New swarms, before being hived, have given up their established location, and two or more of them may be joined together and placed upon any stand desired.

Second swarms are often worth but little, if hived separately. But, if two are united, they will seldom fail to fill their hive and be in good condition for wintering. If queen cells are removed, surplus space given, honey extracted, or empty comb given there is no danger of second swarms.

Swarms issuing the same day will unite peaceably, or a swarm may be joined to another that has been hived three or four days, but, after that, a union is more difficult in the common hive. When such swarms do not issue about the same time, so as to be hived together, let them stand in separate hives till sunset. Then place the one first hived upon a sheet, raising the edge of the hive that the other swarm may enter. Bring the other hive and shake the bees out upon the sheet. If the queen is seen, while the bees are entering, she should be taken away, as the other queen may already have become fertile.

If a colony is found to be queenless in early spring, add its bees to some weak stock having a fertile queen. To do this, sprinkle the bees with diluted honey or water sweetened with sugar, which, at this season, will usually procure them a kind reception.

PREVENTION OF SWARMING.

We have given an easy and certain method to prevent after-swarming, but to prevent the issue of first swarms is sometimes more difficult. Some, who prefer an increased amount of surplus honey to an increase of stocks, effect the object by clipping one of the queen's wings, when she cannot leave with the swarm, and will shortly return to the hive. The queen, however, in attempting to accompany the swarm will usually fall to the ground directly in front of the stand, therefore a broad board should slant from the alighting board to the ground to enable her to crawl back into the hive. When the issue of the swarm is observed the queen should be found and returned, for should she fail to get back the swarm would probably reissue upon the hatching of a young queen. Great care must be taken not to clip the wings of the young queens before they have become fertile, else they will remain barren and worthless. Another way is to examine the combs every ten days while the *swarming fever* lasts and remove all the queen cells. If while doing this, more room be given in the body of the hive by removing a frame of honey, two examinations will usually suffice.

QUIETING AND HANDLING BEES.

Before a swarm issues from a hive, the bees fill their sacs with honey to last while on their journey and aid them in starting in their new home. While thus filled, they are (like a man soon after dinner) uncommonly good natured and obliging, seldom showing any rough *points* of character. Yet, lest some "luckless wight" might have been sleeping on the outside of the hive while its comrades were filling their "jackets" within, we will give the clustered swarm a slight sprinkling with diluted honey or sweetened water. If they were docile and tractable before, they are doubly so now. We may shake them down, hunt out their queen, or perform with them any operation we wish and they will not sting us, unless we compel them by pressure to do so. Here we have the true explanation of all the "charms," "secrets" and "recipes for taming bees," with which unprincipled venders have long humbugged a too credulous public. The whole art of "taming bees" is embodied in the following:

1st. A honey bee filled with "liquid sweets" will not sting of its own accord.

2d. Bees, when frightened, will generally fill themselves with honey, and if given liquid sweets will invariably accept them.

Bees may be frightened thus:

1st. By blowing upon them the smoke of spunk, tobacco or cotton rags.

2d. By confining them to the hive, and rapping the sides of it lightly with a small stick. At first, the bees will try to get

---

NOTE.—Wood nearly rotten we have found to be much better than a roll of cotton rags for smoking bees.

out, but failing will fill themselves with honey.

Formerly small rolls of cotton cloth with tobacco added at times were used for smoking bees, but since the invention of the Bellows Smoker no bee-keeper can afford to be without it. It *will* hold fire for hours from cotton rags, rotten wood or any thing suitable. It is worked with one hand and puffs smoke in dense volumes into the hive or among the combs. On opening a hive puff a little smoke into the entrance and wait a moment for them to fill themselves with honey. If other stocks are close and the bees interfere, blow smoke into the entrance of each hive. Toward fall, when bees have become rich in stores, they are harder to control. They are also more irritable in cool, cloudy weather, which prevents them from visiting the flowers. At such times, a little smoking tobacco scattered upon and rolled up with the rags, will effectually tranquilize them. Or, if addicted to the use of the pipe or cigar, the rags may be saved. In short, by the use of smoke, timely given and repeated as needed, bees may be kept in subjection for any length of time. Some use water, sweetened with sugar or honey. Sugar is preferable as the scent will not so readily attract bees from other hives. Sprinkle it upon the bees with a small clothes broom. Give them time to fill themselves, and they will have no disposition to sting. The sweetened water is very useful in uniting, and for keeping swarms quiet when away from their combs. Although, by using care and gentleness in our manipulations of the hive, the risk of being stung is small, we advise the beginner to use a veil for the face till he has gained courage and experience, when it may be dispensed with. This veil may be a piece of coarse black millinet, fastened to the rim of a summer hat and tucked in about the neck. The rim of the hat holds the veil away from the face, making it safe, cool and comfortable. The cost of the millinet, hat included, is trifling, and several may be trimmed and kept for visitors who wish to view the wonders of the apiary.

For a screen to carry in the pocket, to use when away from home on any kind of hat, get one-and-a-half yards of millinet or any coarse, open stuff. Gather one side of this into a band that will slip over the crown of the hat down to the brim. This may be secured with a string under the vest collar. If the fabric used is dark-colored and very coarse, it will not tire the eyes or scarcely obstruct the vision.

When at work among the bees, avoid making quick motions or jarring the hives. If a bee come buzzing *threateningly* about, never strike, but keep your head bowed and the rim of your hat and your hand will protect your face. A bee flies in a direct line, and will not dive down to come up into the face. Should the bee refuse to leave, walk quietly into the shade of a tree or into a building. The poison of a bee sting may often be neutralized and swelling prevented, by quickly applying strong spirits of hartshorn. Amusing feats may be performed with bees, when filled with sweets, by confining the queen in a small wire-cloth cage and fastening it upon the hair, whiskers or in your hat, when the swarm will harmlessly cluster around their queen.

CHAPTER III.

BEE PASTURAGE AND PRODUCTS.

"*Honey is not made by the bees, but is simply gathered by them from the nectaries of flowers, and from that peculiar deposit on vegetation during summer, called 'honey dew.'*"—DR. KIRTLAND.

HONEY is a liquid sweet secreted by flowers, and is gathered and stored in the combs unchanged by the bees. If a stock of bees be fed on inferior quality of syrup, and the combs examined, it will be found in the cells unchanged. Hence the quality of honey depends upon the flowers from which it is gathered. White clover, linden, raspberries, &c., affording light-colored honey, while buckwheat, poplar, and dandelion, yield that which is darker.

Honey and pollen are supplied by nearly all the flowering trees and plants of the vegetable kingdom. The varieties, in the northern States, which furnish the largest proportion are, first in the spring, the alders, soft maple and willows. These come very early, and, if not cut short by frost, stimulate breeding, and form for the bees an acceptable change from a spare winter diet. There is then, in most places, a scarcity of flowers for about three weeks, when the hard or sugar maple throws out its golden tassels, and the peach, pear, cherry and smaller fruits, rich in honey and bee-bread, extend an invitation which is never slighted by the provident bees. The apple-tree blossoms now afford a real harvest. Raspberries, especially the red varieties, yield an excessive flow of excellent honey. The month of June brings the white clover, which, in the older parts of the country, is usually the chief source of surplus honey, and of great value everywhere. It continues in blossom about two months, yielding large quantities of superior honey. The tulip-tree, by some called poplar, by others, whitewood, blossoms soon after the appearance of the white clover, and secretes much pure saccharine matter, nearly a teaspoonful being often contained in one of its large bell-shaped flowers. We once had an apiary located near the grove of this timber, and every fine morning, during the time it was in blossom, the bees seemed to be swarming over a ten acre field in the direction of the grove. Catnip, borage, strawberries, honeysuckles, mignonette, hoarhound, motherwort, and various kinds of garden flowers, are rich in honey and valuable when in sufficient quantities. The locust tree, either yellow or black, is a great producer of honey, and while in bloom, the bees will swarm around it to the neglect of other flowers. About the first of July, the linden or basswood opens its ten thousand fragrant petals. Where this timber abounds, the bees reap from it a rich harvest. Mustard is, also, an especial favorite. Corn tassels afford much pollen, and vines of the pumpkin, squash, &c., yield honey. In some seasons, what is called "honey dew," makes its appearance on the vegetation. It is usually confined to a few varieties of trees, giving the leaves a glossy appearance, and is sometimes so copious as to make them quite sticky. The dew of each succeeding morning makes it available till a rain dissolves and washes it away.

Buckwheat continues blossoming for from three to five weeks, keeping the bees busily employed, beside enough honey wasting by evaporation to perfume the air for a considerable distance around. A farther supply is furnished by golden-rod, fireweed, English smartweed, asters, and various other fall flowers. We have omitted to mention many trees and plants that are quite as valuable for their honey bearing properties as some of those enumerated.

OVERSTOCKING.

To a person unacquainted with the immense honey resources of our country, a question will naturally arise as to how many stocks of bees may be safely kept at one point, and whether there is not danger of collecting so great a number as to exhaust the natural supplies of honey. In reply, we would say that we believe it possible to overstock a given locality, and yet we have never been able, in our own experience or otherwise, to get sufficient evidence to confirm us in this belief. Mr. H. B. Gifford, in the *Prairie Farmer*, says: "I knew of one neighborhood, east, a thickly settled place, where nearly every family kept from one to fifty swarms. It is said they get as much honey per swarm as they used to when there were but few kept, and a double price for their honey."

At times the supply of honey seems almost inexhaustible During these harvests the flowers secrete honey through the night, which must be gathered in the fore part of the day, or it is lost by evaporation with the noonday sun. Upon this point, Mr. E. T. Sturtevant, an extensive bee-keeper of Northern Ohio, writes as follows: "A kind Providence furnishes this bountiful supply each day, and if workers are not on hand to gather it on that day, it is gone. I have never known a season when this honey harvest did not enable every strong colony, in the course of a few days, to lay up an abundant supply for its own consumption, and a generous surplus for its owner. To secure this result, however, the hives must be abundantly supplied with workers. The whole secret lies in *strong swarms.* The rapidity with which swarms, at this period of the year increase in weight, is surprising, ranging from three to five, ten to fifteen, or even eighteen pounds per day. My own bees, the last season, built combs and stored honey in their surplus boxes only from twelve to fifteen days. The shortest harvest I have ever known. In this short time, many of my swarms collected, in addition to an ample supply for their own consumption, from thirty to thirty-five pounds surplus. The same would have been true had the number of stocks been ten times as great. I am satisfied it makes but little difference how many strong swarms are collected together; a few days will make them all rich."

We visited Mr. Sturtevant's apiary about the time of this writing, and found it to contain something over two hundred swarms. We have seldom kept more than one hundred stocks in one place, preferring to keep them at different points, two or three miles apart, but after all, we believe the question of overstocking to depend in a great measure upon a continuous and abundant supply of flowers, from early spring till Autumn. Where this supply can be had little fear need be entertained of overstocking.

In most places, there are, even in the best honey years, times of scarcity, during which few flowers can be found. These vacancies may be profitably filled and immense stores of honey secured by planting out flower-trees, shrubs, and cultivating field crops with especial reference to this object.

For bee pasturage, as well as for fruit, the cherry tree has never been rightly appreciated. Several of the early improved varieties bloom in a time when most needed by the bees, and even the latest are fully improved by them. The raspberry continues in bloom about three weeks, and few flowers furnish so large a quantity of purest nectar. The fruit is a surer crop even than the cherry, and every one knows that "purple cane," "black cap" and "orange" raspberries, and "sweet cherries," do not always need to be taken to market to find purchasers.

Let your lanes and avenues and the front of your grounds be lined with the locust, linden, hard and soft maple, tulip and chestnut. These are beautiful shade and ornamental trees and will increase the value of your property ten times the expense of planting them. A pleasing contrast is produced by interspersing among them cherry, apple and other fruit trees, all affording large supplies of delicious honey.

CULTIVATING HONEY CROPS.

White clover stands first on the list of honey crops. When sown with other grasses it is valuable for hay, and for pasture it cannot be excelled. Where it is abundant there are never bees enough to collect one-fourth of the honey it affords. Red clover secretes much honey, yet it is mostly beyond the reach of the common bees, but Italian bees store honey from it to a much greater extent, though chiefly from the smaller blossoms, and the second growth or aftermath. Mustard is one of the most profitable crops to cultivate, as well for its seed as a pasture for bees. It should be thinly sown, and lightly brushed in during April or May, upon good soil, and cut rather green to avoid waste by shelling. It yields from ten to fifteen bushels per acre, and sells readily to manufacturers in large cities at a high price. Even an acre or two of mustard is of great advantage to an apiary, as it keeps branching and blossoming nearly all summer. In most parts of the country there is a dearth of flowers from the fall of the apple-tree blossoms till white clover comes in. To fill this vacancy a plat of turnips may be sown each year. Gather the largest for market or to feed to the stock, and enough small ones will remain in the ground to run to seed the next year, to make a rich pasture for the bees in the most critical part of the season, greatly favoring the advent of early swarms. The value of a field of buckwheat for both bread and honey is well known. In speaking of it as a honey crop, Mr. Harbison says: "When the weather is favorable the bees store honey from it very rapidly, faster at times than they can build combs to receive it. I have seen them fill pieces of old comb, laid close to the entrance of the hive, with honey, and have known colonies to fill four boxes of honey, or about fifty pounds during the continuance of buckwheat. This is by no means an uncommon occurrence, and goes to show that this honey harvest is one of great importance to the bee-keeper. Buckwheat may be sown about a month earlier than usual, to furnish pasturage, to come in about the close of clover to great advantage."

We would add that where linden or basswood abounds it is unnecessary to sow buckwheat (except that sown very early) before the middle of June, but where this timber is scarce sow some the first of June. Mr. Harbison continues: "It is much easier to cultivate and produce enough pasturage, in addition to that from natural sources, to supply one hundred hives of bees than it is to provide pasturage for one hundred head of sheep, and the profit on bees will more than double that of sheep."

Thus far we have only advocated the cultivation of such crops for bees as are also valuable for their grain or seed, our object being to fill with the greatest profit, the vacancies between natural supplies and afford the bees an uninterrupted succession of flowers in greatest abundance from spring to fall. These vacancies mostly occurring when the weather is unusually warm and pleasant, the bees, if supplied with flowers, have every facility for increasing their stores. Catnip will well repay cultivation for honey alone. It continues to blossom for a long time, the bees working upon it with the greatest assiduity "from early morn till dewy eve."

POLLEN

Pollen, or bee-bread, is the fertilizing dust, or fine meal-like substance discharged by the anthers of flowers. It is used for feeding the young and immature bees, great quantities being collected for this purpose and carried to the hives in little balls or pellets upon the thighs of the workers. Pollen is furnished by different species of flowers of almost every variety and shade of color, the most common being yellow. This has caused some to mistake these little yellow pellets for wax, to be used in comb building. Such should observe that just as much pollen is taken to hives already filled with comb, as to any others. In order to stimulate breeding in early spring, unbolted flour is sometimes used as a substitute for pollen. The bees will not accept it unless given before much natural pollen can be had. Where snow prevents flowers starting until long after the bees begin to fly, such feeding should not be neglected, especially in large apiaries. It will prevent robbing, strengthen the stocks, and encourage habits of industry. Unbolted rye flour is best, but bolted flour may be used if mixed with sawdust or cut straw. If spread on boards, with strips tacked on the edges to prevent waste, and placed in some sunny corner out of the wind, the bees will work upon it quite freely.

PROPOLIS OR BEE GLUE.

This is a resinous gum collected by the bees from the leaves, buds and trunks of trees and plants, and is used for coating over uneven surfaces, and for filling holes and cracks within the hive. When cold, it is very hard and brittle, being quite a different substance from wax of which the combs are composed. Thus we find honey, pollen and propolis the only substances *gathered* by the bees.

WAX AND COMB BUILDING.

As animals must be fed large quantities of grain to enable them to secrete a few pounds of fat, so bees, on a like principle, consume from fifteen to twenty-five pounds of honey, (Dr. Kirtland says twenty-five,) for the production of a single pound of wax. The wax exudes from the rings or folds of the abdomen of the worker, forming thin flakes or scales, which are removed as fast as formed and used for constructing combs. It takes about two and a half pounds of wax to fill a hive of ordinary size with comb. By confining a swarm of bees in a movable-comb hive and feeding them, the bees will build comb, consuming about twenty pounds of sweet to produce one pound of comb or wax. It will readily be seen that wax is by far the most expensive article used by the bees. The time spent in constructing the comb should also be taken into the account, which, if occupied in gathering honey, would, at this season of the year, enable them to store much more, and making the cost of a pound of comb equivalent to at least twenty-five pounds of honey. This honey, at twenty-five cents per pound, would give us six dollars and twenty-five cents as the cost of a pound of comb. Good combs melted into wax and taken to market might bring forty cents per pound, which, deducted from the cost price, would show a loss of five dollars and eighty-five cents on every pound of wax sold. These estimates show that the bee-keeper cannot afford to melt down any combs that can be used to advantage by the bees. Even drone comb, if not *too* dark colored, should be used in the surplus boxes. If first swarms are put into hives furnished with empty combs, they will often fill them in an incredible short time, and swarm the same season. For saving all good pieces of comb, whether large or small, movable-frame hives are indispensable. In filling up an empty frame lay it upon a table or board, and fasten in the combs by dipping an edge of each piece into melted comb. The scraps may be melted and should not be very hot. It soon cools, leaving the combs firmly attached. Frames when thus filled may be given to strong colonies in exchange for frames of honey. Stocks kept supplied in this way through the gathering season, will store astonishing quantities of honey, and in autumn, if any lack provisions for winter, it is easy to give them some of the full combs previously removed.

HOW TO SECURE STRAIGHT COMBS.

The *full* advantage of the movable-comb principle is only secured by having *worker* comb built *within all* the frames. Upon the first introduction of movable frames, bee-keepers often failed to prevent the bees from building their combs across the frames, as many yet do, and until recently but few attempted to prevent the bees from building drone comb. Sometimes strips of comb are attached to the under side of the top bars of the frames. This is a very good practice, as it gives the bees a start *within* the frames with *worker* comb. The difficulty of obtaining comb for the purpose, especially in long strips, made it necessary to use a wooden guide, and it was discovered that the bees were more certain to follow the guides by elevating the rear end of the hive. The best way to secure straight combs is by placing each empty frame between two full ones. If no full ones are on hand; use comb foundation, which if used altogether in the brood nest will prevent the building of much drone comb.

HOW TO SECURE STRAIGHT COMBS.

Bees will commence working on foundation combs, made of pure beeswax, much sooner than on old combs, and all the cells being worker size, drone comb will be entirely prevented, but in warm weather when a large swarm is introduced into a hive filled with foundation the heat sometimes becomes so great as to cause the foundations to sag; to entirely overcome this objection, we recommend the following, from Mr. W. Davidson, of Brooklyn:

"Punch two holes with an awl in both the top and bottom bar of the frame, exactly opposite each other. Put No. 24 annealed wire through these holes, passing it along the top bar and twisting the ends together at the bottom. Cut the foundation to fit the frame loosely, leaving one-eighth inch on each side and bottom. Have some wax kept just melted by a lamp. Lay the foundation aginst the wires, and shove it closely aginst the top bar. Now pour a spoonful of wax against the foundation at one end of of the top bar, and quickly tip up the frame so that it will run to the other end, and the work is done.

"For neatness in handling press the foundation close to the wires and fasten it in a couple of places with a drop of wax from a brush. I doubt if foundation can be fastened by any other method more rapidly."

We have tried this device of Mr. Davidson, and have visited his apiary to see how the wires worked. It seems to us that this settles the question of sagging.

We are now trying some frames with the wires waxed, and pressing them close against the foundation, we think one will not be able to tell where the wires cross. Another advantage of this process is that the wires hold the top bars of the frames so tightly that they never will be pulled off, which sometimes happens where they are only nailed.

REMOVING DEFECTIVE COMBS.

Certain persons would have us deprive our bees of their combs every two or three years, and compel them to build anew. This we consider a useless waste of the time and material of the bees, for although every litter of brood leaves a cocoon or thin lining in each cell, the cells were large at first, and the cocoons are so thin that after the lapse of ten years no perceptible difference can be seen in the size of the bees, the combs meanwhile becoming warmer and safer for the swarm in winter. The above practice is universally condemned by our best practical apiarians. One of them, while advocating the removal of worthless or defective combs, says:

"What old bee-keeper has not had abundant proof that stocks eight or ten years old, or even older, are often among the very best in his whole apiary." Stocke says he saw a colony which he was assured had "swarmed annually for forty-six years."

The common practice of some bee-keepers, of breaking out the lower combs from common hives, if the combs happen to be dark colored, is to be discouraged, for when done in early spring the stock that year will often fail to be productive either of swarms or surplus honey. Yet when movable frames are used, if healthy stocks and early and vigorous swarms are desired, we should make a general examination as soon as spring has fairly opened, and place every stock upon a fair footing for the work of the season. Portions of the comb are liable to become useless from various causes. If the hive was not properly ventilated, the lower edges of combs may be mouldy. The brood combs may contain old sour bee-bread, which the bees are unable to remove, and this is a frequent cause of failure. There may be a great excess of drone-comb. If combs are defective in any of these points, trim off so much as is defective and *no more*. In the Eastern States, where the disease called "foul brood" is known, the bees of the diseased stock must be driven from their combs into an empty box, letting them remain without combs thirty-six hours, till free from the honey taken with them, when they may be put into a *new* hive and fed in the chamber if necessary. Carefully keep the honey from the bees, else other stocks will contract the disease. If heated to the boiling point, it is said, the honey will be harmless and may be used for feeding. The disease has never been known west of the State of New York, bee-keepers having been careful about obtaining bees from infected districts.

MELTING COMBS INTO WAX.

All *waste* combs should be rendered into wax, by crowding them into a sack made of coarse open cloth and placing it in a kettle of boiling water. Continue to press it with a hoe, removing the wax as it rises to the top. Wax may be bleached perfectly white by forming it into thin flakes, by pouring it upon the surface of tepid water and afterwards spreading it upon canvas, out of doors.

If many hives are kept, it pays well to have a wax extractor. It is very convenient to hold and drain the caps in extracting, (See "Wax Extractors" page 53).

CHAPTER IV.

THE EXTRACTOR—COMB-FOUNDATION—SURPLUS HONEY IN BOXES AND EXTRACTED—MARKETING HONEY.

THE HONEY EXTRACTOR.

SURPLUS HONEY IN BOXES AND EXTRACTED.

The great object of the beekeeper is to secure surplus honey. All management of bees should look toward securing the greatest amount of honey in the best shape for use and for market.

To this end the Extractor, Comb-foundation, and boxes of uniform size are now essentials.

The Extractor, invented by Herr von Hruschka, a German, residing in Venice, Italy, is a simple instrument, consisting of a cylinder and a revolving basket to hold the frame, and a faucet below to draw off the honey. It is thrown from the comb by centrifugal force and the emptied comb returned to the hive to be refilled. It is best that the basket alone revolve and not the cylinder. It is turned by a simple gearing at the top. The straight wire sides of the basket support the comb and prevent it from breaking.

Two combs, hung in opposite sides of the basket balance each other. The honey is thrown from one side by a few turns of the machine, after which reverse the sides of the comb and in the same way extract from the other.

A little practice will teach one how hard to turn to extract the honey and after a little experience one can soon learn how swift to turn in warm weather so as to throw out the honey from combs containing larvæ without dislodging the bees. However, we would not advise extracting from combs which contain much larvæ.

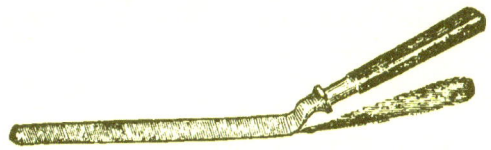

UNCAPPING KNIFE.

When honey is capped over, the caps must be shaved off with a sharp knife before extracting. The handle of the knife should be bent so that the fingers clasped around it will not be in the way in using the knife. The blade will run better if the honey be frequently wiped off with a warm rag, and especial care be taken that no wax stick to it.

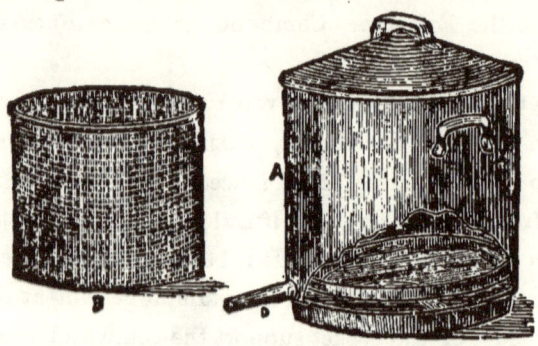

BEES-WAX EXTRACTOR.

The Wax Extractor kept at hand, is an excellent thing in which to scrape the caps from the knife. It is readily closed up to keep out insects, the honey drains off and can be saved, and the clippings are ready in it without any handling for melting into wax.

Honey is not fully ripe until it is sealed over. If extracted before it is sealed over it will sometimes sour when put immediately into close vessels. It should be kept open to ripen by evaporation for a time. A better way is this: after extracting honey, let it stand for some hours in a large vessel having a cock at the bottom. The thin watery honey which rises should be fed to the bees. The heavy ripe honey will settle to the bottom.

It should be drawn off by a cock from the bottom of the vessel and canned or put up in barrels or jars for market. Before using barrels they should be coated inside with melted bees-wax, or paraffine to prevent the honey from being tainted and also to prevent leakage. It is done by pouring a gallon or so of hot wax into the barrel when dry and warm. It is rinsed around quickly so that the whole surface is covered and poured out to be used again. When packed directly for market nice pound bottles put up in crates of from two to four dozen will be most salable. Grocers can readily handle it in this shape. In some places it is just as salable in self sealing fruit jars. If found to be so it is easily put up in this way.

The Extractor is a necessary article in every apiary for many reasons. In good honey harvests, bees will often fill up the brood nest with honey so that there is little room left for the queen to lay eggs. When this is done the bees necessarily dwindle and sometimes become so weak as to be unfit to keep over winter. Whereas by extracting the honey from the combs the queen has room to lay eggs, the bees are stimulated to greater activity, and the hive is kept strong for future work. By extracting freely during a honey harvest far more honey can be secured than otherwise, because the bees are thus kept working at their best all the time. Again, much honey will will be stored in the broodnest in the fall when they will not make comb or store honey in surplus boxes. Unless honey is plentiful in the fields, extracting should be done in a closed room from which bees are excluded.

It is best to have an extra set of combs in extracting, and open a hive but once, smoking it well if the bees are cross. As the frames are removed one by one into a carrying-box, the empty ones should take their places, and the hive be closed up.

COMB-FOUNDATION.

Bees consume much honey in building comb. They cannot store honey, or raise brood, without it; and when left to build it they will not begin to build until the honey harvest opens. A farmer may succeed, if he has hands sufficient, in housing a good crop, though he has tools and fences to make, and granaries to build after the seeding time opens, but with the same help he cannot secure and house as much as when the necessary implements are ready at hand. So bees will gather honey and develop much more rapidly when they have comb ready at hand when the harvest opens. Sometimes, if left to themselves, they build so much drone comb that, unless the hives are watched and the drone comb removed, a large lot of useless drones are reared at quite a cost of time and honey.

Hence beekeepers have long felt the need of some way of furnishing hives with comb already built. Attempts were made, but not until recently was a machine perfected which fully answered the purpose of making artificial comb-foundation. By it sheets

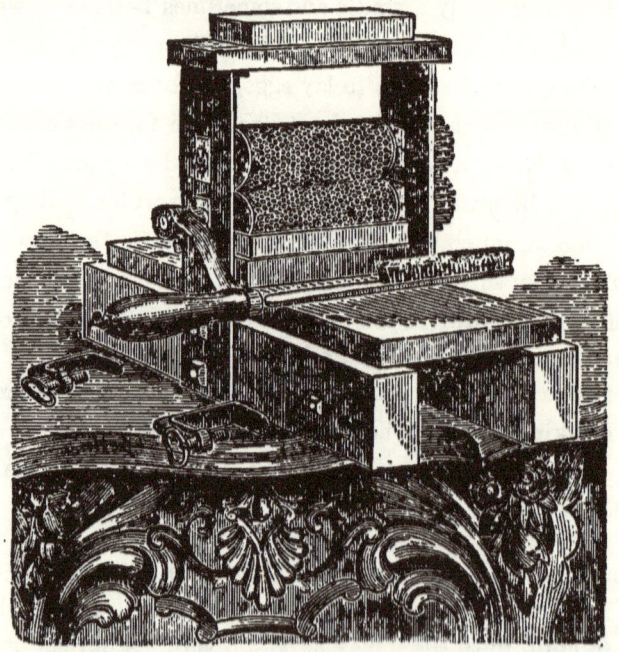

COMB-FOUNDATION MACHINE.

of pure wax are impressed with the exact shape of the bottoms and beginning of the side-walls of the cells. Bees readily accept them and lengthen out the walls of the cells. These sheets of comb-foundation are very useful in the brood-nest. They answer best when they contain five or six square feet to the pound. They are fastened to the top bars in different ways. Some lay a sheet flat on the top bar with the edge near the edge of the bar, and smooth it down firmly to the wood with a piece of iron, then tack a narrow strip over this into the top bar and bend it at right angles so as to hang in the centre of the frame. It should not come within less than half an inch of each end and bottom of the frame. Others fasten them simply with the strip; but perhaps the best way is to fasten them in small grooves made in the under side of the top bar with white glue or wax. Wax is preferable.

In the broodnest comb-foundation is exceedingly useful. Sometimes bees accept it almost immediately, and within twenty-four hours the beginning of the side-walls are lengthened into walls of cells, and the queen busy laying eggs in them. They should be made of pure bees-wax and not of paraffine or ceresin. They are especially useful in securing fall honey where it is abundant. If the full combs for winter use are set away and comb-foundation or empty comb inserted, bees will work with marvelous rapidity. At the close of the harvest they can be removed and the sealed honey returned for the winter. Sometimes this late fall honey is very nice in flavor and appearance. The sheets if used in surplus boxes should be thinner than those in the broodnest because sometimes bees will not thin them as they do at others.

By using strips of comb-foundation in boxes or section-frames bees are stimulated to work on them more rapidly than otherwise, and honey combs more regular in appearance are obtained.

HONEY BOXES.

The size and shape of honey boxes should be modified on one hand by the habits of the bee, and on the other by the demands of trade.

Boxes should be of uniform size so as to be interchangeable and so as to be packed for market in crates of uniform size.

Formerly long low and wide boxes were used and these taken off and sent to market just as they were without separating the combs. This mode was found very objectionable because the package was too large for convenient retail trade, and because the honey must be cut up to get at small quantities. This breaking up of honey causes great loss, daubs up the store, and drawes flies so that many grocerymen decidedly object to handling it.

Later, section boxes were prefered which had little grooves through which the grocer could split them up into boxes containing single combs. These answered better but sometimes combs will be built irregularly in them unless separators are used. Separate sections with glass on each side are popular in some sections, but consumers will soon tire of paying for unnecessary glass. So too, by some, boxes with four sides of glass are advocated. They supply a demand where there is a sufficient call for fancy styles as will pay the extra prices. Honey may be secured in various fancy shapes, hearts, circles, &c., and sold to confectioners for weddings and other extra occasions at a great price. This is done by cutting the holes in plank or sections and placing them in frames in the hive. Bees will fill tumblers and glass jars of any shape if a piece of comb be attached for a commencement, and they are put over the cluster in time. They should be put on early to be nicely filled with pure white honey.

But aside from fancy purposes the great mass of honey must be put up in small convenient packages to suit the retail trade in order to increase consumption. Bees alone can pack comb nicely in boxes so as to prevent waste. In other pursuits a "middle man" does the packing and preparing for the retail market. Here the bee-keeper must make his bees do it. Boxes should contain but a single comb and from one to three pounds of honey, In some places the smaller boxes retail best, in others the larger. Other things being equal bees store honey better in a two or three pound box than in one smaller though they will start well in smaller ones if they are arranged in a large frame so that the bees and air can pass freely from one to another. Small boxes have this advantage—that when placed at the side of the brood nest, the queen is not apt to lay eggs in them. Perhaps the size of box which one adopts should be regulated to some extent by the size of the hive he is using. Two tiers of boxes may be placed in the brood nest in wide frames and in these from two to four boxes long according to size of the hive. Thus a large frame to fit the broodnest will hold from four to eight of the small ones. There may be either two tiers of the wide frames holding the boxes, or two tiers of boxes in one wide frame. If the caps are shallower than the broodnest the cases should be half the depth of the frame and hold one tier of the boxes. Bees store honey more rapidly in the broodnest, at times than in the cap, but they will seal it up more rapidly above. Strips of tin one-half inch narrower than the inside depth of the honey box should be tacked on one side of the wide frames so as to prevent the passage of bees above and below. Bees will not attach comb to tin, and by its use straight combs are gotten in the frames which will pack closely without mashing, The tops and sides of the wide frame which holds the boxes should be two inches wide and fit closely together in the hive. The bottom should be one and three-fourths wide and tacked in the centre at the bottom so that when two are used side by side bees can enter from below between them. For the same reason both the bottom and top of the boxes should be one and three-fourths inches wide and the sides two inches. If desired boxes thus arranged may be covered with glass after they are taken from the hive. The glass is fastened in by tin tacks driven into the top and bottom and bent over it.

The best mode of management seems to be that which will enable the bee-keeper to place boxes in the broodnest, separated from it by a wire cloth division board if they are of large size, and so arranged that when full they may be removed to the upper chamber to be capped over, and empty combs with starters of comb-foundation put in their places. When boxes are not used at the sides of the broodnest two tiers should at times be used in the upper box. When the boxes in the first tier are nearly full and much of it sealed over remove the wide frames containing them, bees and all, after smoking them well, and place frames full of empty boxes in there places; giving entrance through the tops of two or three to the full ones, which should be placed above them. This will prevent the difficulty often experienced of getting bees to work in empty boxes when full ones are removed. By the time the upper tier of boxes are finished the lower one will generally be half or 'two-thirds full. The upper tier of boxes may now be removed without trouble and stored away, and the lower tier again raised and other empty ones with starters of comb-foundation put in their places. This does not necessitate entering the body of the hive and the more timid may follow it with success. A very good plan when the bee-keeper has not time to manipulate, is to use section boxes held together with strips of manilla paper.

Comb-honey must be preserved from worms after it is taken from the hive. In warm weather many worms will hatch upon it and as they feed entirely on wax, they will, if unmolested, eat off the wax which seals the honey and cause it to trickle down in a very unmarketable condition. This can be prevented by placing the box honey when removed in a small *warm* room or box where the miller eggs will hatch, and smoking them well with brimstone two or three times at intervals of twelve or fifteen days, using at the rate of a pound of sulphur for every 250 to 300 cubic feet contained in the room or box.

MARKETING HONEY.

Honey, like other products, must generally be sold in quantities to wholesale men who distribute it according to the necessities of trade. These wholesale merchants, can themselves repack extracted honey, yet as they are apt to adulterate it, the bee-keeper himself should pack in small parcels with from two to four dozen jars in a case, to suit the trade, placing his own name and apiary on each jar and also labeling it as to its source and quality.

It is more important that comb honey should be packed to suit the retail trade, because only bees can properly arrange and secure it. The combs should be in small frames or boxes two inches wide and containing from one to three pounds. Glass may be added at the sides or not according to the demands of the market. These boxes should be packed in crates holding from two to four dozen according to size.

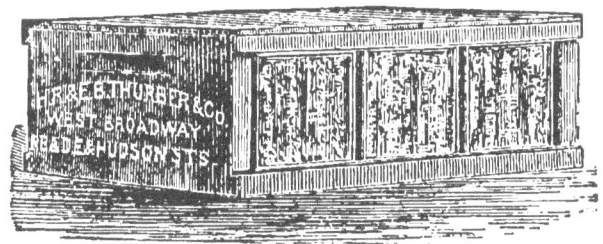

HONEY CRATE.

The crates should be made in the simplest way. The two ends should be of seven-eighths of an inch boards, one-fourth inch longer and deeper than the measurement of the boxes to be inserted. Two strips from seven-eighths to one and one-half inches wide as best suits the glass to be used, between are nailed on each side one at the top and the other at the bottom. These strips have a rabbet made for glass on one edge. They are nailed two on each side even with the top and bottom of the ends Glass of the proper size is slipped into the grooves and secured by tin tacks driven into the end pieces and bent over the glass. The bottom and top are made by nailing or screwing on one-half inch boards. These crates just answer the purpose of the retail dealer. The honey is shown through the glass, and the lid keeps out flies and insects. These crates may be returned if sold to a grocer near by and refilled the next year. With rubber tubing tacked around the crate they may be shipped anywhere with perfect safety. But perhaps a better and cheaper spring is made by placing the crate in an extra box with small wire coil springs on each side.

USES OF HONEY.

From time immemorial honey has held an important position among useful products. In the Bible it is used to illustrate the highest spiritual enjoyments. The judgments of the Lord are said to be "sweeter also than honey and the honey comb."

In ancient times honey was not only used as an article of diet but held also an important place among medicines. In this age of chemistry and new and patent medicines, almost any one of which will cure any disease from toothache to cancer or consumption, the virtues of such an old fashioned article as honey are almost lost sight of; but when quackery shall have had its day, it will again be found, we believe, that there is great virtue in honey, especially in diseases affecting the lungs and throat.

Many of the old doctor books give receipts for the medical use of honey. In the Paris catalogue of edibles and drinkables says John Hunter; in his "Manual of Bee-Keeping:" "Were shown honey-bread, spiced bread, fruits preserved in honey, jellies, sweetmeats, cakes, bon bons, pastiles, and chocolates, whilst for *eau de vie* we need not leave old England, seeing it is made both from honey and wax. Then we have hydromel, or metheglin, champagne, red and white wines, liquors, fruit syrups, vinegar and fruit cordials. This is a pretty list of delicacies for our housewives to exercise their ingenuity and skill upon. Regretfully I say I have no knowledge how to make most of these good things." He thus describes the process of making metheglin: "When the comb has been drained of its honey, put it in a large vessel, then pour in sufficient luke warm water to swim it nicely. Let it stand two days, stir occasionally, then strain it. Skim the scum from the liquor carefully, filter the sediment through a flannel, then boil one hour. To three gallons add two pounds of raisins, one ounce ground ginger, and seven or eight laurel leaves, then cool. Add a little brewers' yeast, let it stand part of a day, then barrel it, leaving the barrel open for two or three days; bung it up and let it remain untouched for six months, then bottle it. * * The longer it is kept the better it will be." If an egg will float on the liquor it will be about the right strength. Metheglin may of course be made from run honey, but by soaking the combs in water we utilize the honey which would otherwise be lost. A little lump of sugar put in each bottle will make it as fine as brandy.

Honey vinegar is made as follows: Put a half pound of honey to a quart of water, boiling hot; mix well, and expose to the greatest heat of the sun without closing the vessel containing it, but sufficiently so to keep out insects. In about six weeks this liquor becomes acid and changes to strong vinegar of an excellent quality.

Honey is prescribed by the medical council of Great Britain for use in the following pharmaceutical preparations, viz.: Confection of pepper, confection of scammony, confection of turpentine, honey and borax, oxymel of squills, and simple oxymel. It is used in various medical preparations also. In America increasing attention is being given to the medical properties of honey.

HONEY CAKE, No. 1—John Hunter's.—"Mix a quart of strained honey with a half pound of powdered white sugar, half a pound of fresh butter and the juice of two oranges or lemons. Warm these ingredients slightly, just enough to soften the butter, and then stir the mixture very hard, adding a grated nutmeg. Mix in gradually two pounds or less of sifted flour, make it into a dough just stiff enough to roll out easily and beat it well all over with a rolling pin, then roll it out into a large sheet half an inch thick, cut it into round cakes with the top of a tumbler dipped frequently in flour, lay them in shallow tin pans, slightly buttered and bake them."

HONEY CAKES, No. 2.—Soak three cups of dried apples over night; chop slightly and simmer in two coffee cups of honey for two hours, then add one and a half coffee cups of honey, one half coffee cup of sugar, one coffee cup of melted butter, three eggs, two teaspoons saleratus, cloves, cinnamon, powdered lemon or orange peel, and ginger syrup, if you have it. Mix all together, add the apples and thin flour enough for a stiff batter. Bake in a slow oven. This will make two good sized cakes.

HONEY CAKES, No. 3—Muth's.—One gallon of honey, (dark honey is best,) fifteen eggs, three pounds of sugar, (a little more honey in its place may be better), one and a half ounces of baking soda, two ounces of hartshorn, two pounds of almonds (chopped up), two pounds of citron, four ounces of cinnamon, two ounces of cloves, two ounces of mace, eighteen pounds of flour. Let the honey come to almost a boil; then let it cool off again and add the ingredients. Cut out and bake. The cakes are iced afterward with sugar and the white of eggs.

HONEY PUDDING.—Three pints thinly sliced apples, one pint of honey one pint of corn meal, small piece of butter, one teaspoonful soda, the juice of two lemons and their grated rinds. Stir the dry soda into the honey, then add the apples, melted butter and a little salt; now, add the lemon rind and juice and at once stir in the flour. Bake one hour. Serve hot or cold with sauce.

Honey Mead is a drink which is becoming popular in some of our cities within the past few years. We do not favor drinking, but if men must drink something, we think the more innocent the drink the better for them.

CITY BEE-KEEPING.

In the whole round of natural history, nothing is more interesting than the study of the honey bee. Not only those who live in the country, but almost anywhere in our land, a few bees may be kept with pleasure and profit. A single hive, with an "Observing Hive" filled from it in the summer and placed in the parlor (see "Observing Hive") will furnish means to test and study the curious things about the bee.

Not only is this true in our smaller towns and smaller cities, but even in the heart of our largest cities, bees will find pasturage among the millions of flowers that bloom under every window that decks the lawns and gardens and walks, and from many of the maple, locusts and other shade trees along the streets and parks. Besides, bees will fly three or four miles for pasturage with profit.

Mr. W. J. Pettitt has, for a number of years, conducted successfully an apiary of some fifty or sixty hives of bees in the heart of the city of Dover, England, which find a good living and a surplus for the owner among the innumerable flowers of various species that fringe the jutting edges of the white cliffs about Dover

Mr. Charles F. Muth, well known to the apiarians of the West, has, for several years, kept an apiary in the city of Cincinnati; which, we believe, numbers between twenty and thirty hives. He is quite an enthusiast, and finds them very interesting and profitable.

Being perfectly satisfied of the feasibility of city beekeeping, we have procured a large number of bees, and through courtesy of Mr. Holland, president of the American Express Company, we have established an interesting apiary upon the roof of their large building, 61 Hudson street, New York, in the management of which we anticipate much pleasure. We have no fears as to the source of their supplies, and we recommend beekeeping as a profitable industry, to assist many families in this, and the outskirts of other towns where there is space for placing them.

It was the opinion of Huish, a distinguished English writer on bees, in 1817, that within the circumference of ten miles of London, ample provision might be found for the support of ten thousand hives. Since that time developments of this industry show that he has underrated rather than overrated the capacity for bees, especially when applied to our land of flowers.

THE BEE-KEEPING INDUSTRY.

Palestine was called "a land that floweth with milk and honey," and with more truth, may the same be applied to our own country. Until two centuries ago, honey held its place as the great sweet of the world. The art of refining sugar, caused it to be left far behind, because the beekeeper still pursued the old plan of annually murdering his faithful workers, to get their stores.

Honey has ever been considered of great medicinal power in certain classes of diseases, and is very palatable to a large proportion of people, but the small supply of the article and the inferiority of that which under old methods of squeezing and draining from the mashed combs caused it to fall into comparative disuse. But within a generation greater strides have been made in the development of this industry than in any other. Sugar can be produced and refined only with a great amount of capital, but every family throughout the land can help to swell the products of this industry and the number of both large and small bee-keepers is increasing with amazing rapidity. Even the cotton gin added no more to its appropriate industry than has the various improvements of movable comb hives, extractors, comb-foundation, queen rearing, wax machines, smokers, modes of wintering and means of protecting the person from stings, added to the bee-keeping industry. We cannot too strongly reiterate the absolute necessity now for these improvements. To do without them now, in bee-culture is as bad as the man who attempts to "seed cotton" for a living in these days of cotton gins and steam manufacturing mills.

In speaking of this great industry we know not hardly where to begin. There are now three or four magazines devoted exclusively to the subject. Many bee-keepers' conventions, State, local, and national, have

FOR THE BEGINNER.

Inasmuch as there are many questions which beginners ask, we propose in this article to be more explicit for their benefit, than we would be to advanced apiarists., especially in the explanation of words and implements used in modern bee-keeping.

The word bee, is of good old Anglo-Saxon origin, and we like it. *Apis* is the Latin word meaning *a bee*, from which we get the word *apiary*, meaning *a place where bees are kept; apiarian* meaning *one who keeps*

VIEW OF OUR HOME APIARY AT NEVADA, OHIO, 1869.

bees; and *api culture*, which is the same as bee-culture. We sometimes see the word "*mel-extractor.*" *Mel* is the Latin word for *honey*. Hence, *mel-extractor* means honey-extractor; and "*apis-melifica*" means *the honey making bee.* This term is applied especially to the black bee in natural history, whilst others are distinguished by some local adjective as *apis ligustica*, meaning the ligurian, or Italian bee.

If you watch a hive of bees in spring, you will see many coming in with little balls on their hind legs. Some of them yellow and some of other colors. Some ignorant people suppose that this is wax. It is pollen, or powdered farina, gathered from the stamens of flowers. It is of very disagreable taste, and care should be taken that none be mixed

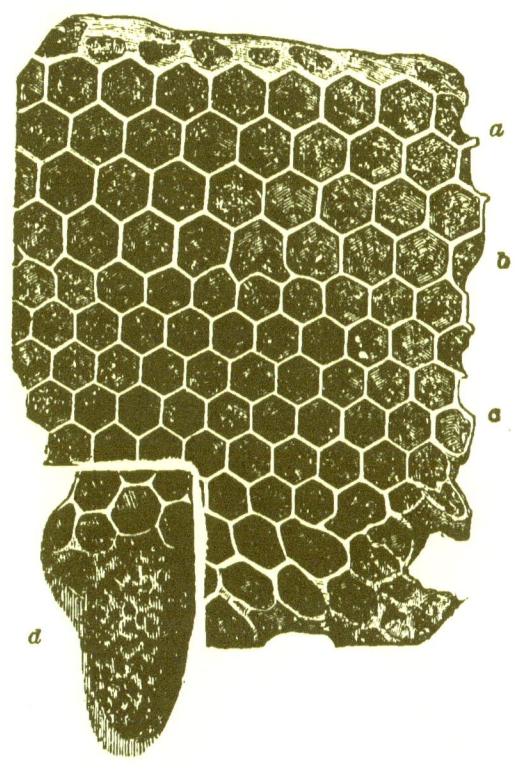

HONEY-COMB.

a—Drone-cells. c—Worker-cells.
b—Deformed-cells. d—Queen-cell.

with our honey. It is used largely in rearing young bees On opening a hive, you will often find it stuck tight with some dark colored sticky stuff, that gums your hand on handling the frames. It is *"propolis"* a glue obtained from certain plants, which bees use for gluing up all crevices and making the hive tight. Drones and queen bees do not sting. They may be handled with impunity. Only worker bees sting. A little experience will enable you to tell the loud coarse buzzing sound of a flying drone from the softened hum of the worker. And the keen mad hum, when about to sting, is easily distinguished from the gentle hum of a worker bee when attending to his regular duties. You should examine some comb and learn to tell the difference between worker comb, in which an inch measures across the top of five cells, whilst four drone cells measure an inch in the same way.

Honey will be put in either, and sometimes the cells are considerably lengthened out to hold honey. If the walls of cells are broken off, bees will soon build them up when honey is gotten.

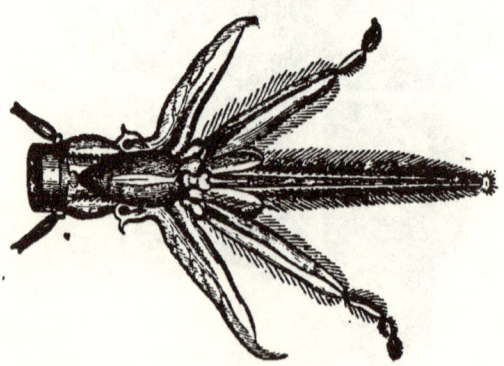

BEE'S TONGUE.

The antennæ of a bee are two little organs sticking up like horns, on the front of the head, sometimes called "feelers." They seem to be the organs of touch, and are the means of intercommunication of knowledge The ligula, commonly called the tongue, is folded when at rest. but when at work it is darted rapidly among the flowers; receives the honey and conveys it to the honey-sacs, from which it is emptied into the cells. The engraving shows how the tongue appears when magnified. *A* is the hollow tube through which the sweet juice or honey is sucked. The reported division of the tube into three parts stated by naturalists, is corroborated by the longitudinal line seen under the lens. The other large appendages shown, appear to be feet for enabling the bee to support itself while sucking up the nectar, and also for enabling it to back out after getting all it wants.

The sting is often the dread of beginners. It is composed of two darts in one sheath. These darts when inserted into the flesh penetrate

BEE-STING.

alternately, till the whole sting is buried. Each is furnished with barbs, which retain it until the poison escapes. The poison bag lies near the root of the sting, and the poison is ejected along the barbed darts into the wound. When stung remove the sting by rubbing it outward, and not by catching it between the thumb and finger, because in this way all the poison is pressed from the bag into the wound and the effect is much severer than it otherwise would be. After extracting the sting, pinch or press the wound and apply some alkali, as soda or hartshorn.

QUEEN CELL AND LARVÆ.

In brood rearing remember that queens hatch in about fourteen days from the egg; workers in about twenty-one; and drones in about twenty-four days. Any worker egg may be used by the bees in rearing a queen. If the egg is hatched before it is used by the bees, the queen may emerge in less than fourteen days. The queen lays eggs very rapidly, sometimes as many as 2,000 or 3,000 per day. She bends her body, in laying and leaves the small white egg, sticking to the bottom of the cell. In the accompanying figure at *b b* eggs are shown

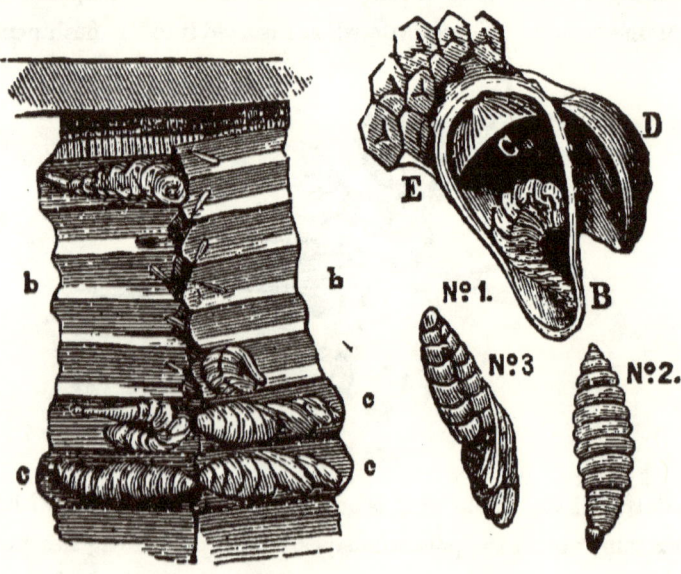

at the bottom of the cell, and larvæ in different stages at *c c*. No. 1 represents a queen-cell cut open, to show its construction. It is attached to the comb at *e*. The part removed is shown at *d*; the queen larvæ at *b*, and the royal jelly at *c*. No. 2. shows one of the larvæ taken from its cell. And No. 3. the same just before it begins to spin its cocoon.

SURPLUS HONEY IN BOXES AND EXTRACTED. 81

The queen lays the *egg*; after it is hatched it is a little worm, grub, or maggot, called a *larva* for five or six days. The bees then cover the cell and the larvæ spins around itself a silken covering called a cocoon.

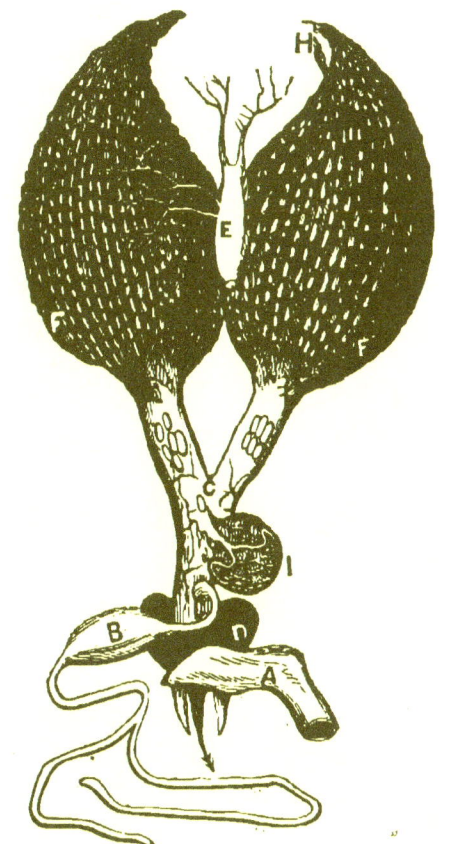

THE OVARIES OF THE QUEEN BEE.

After this it is called a *nymph*, *pupa*, or *chrysalis*, when the proper time arrives, it comes forth from the cell, a perfect bee. The cocoon is left as a lining in the cell when a bee hatches. This makes old combs much stronger than new ones.

Perhaps the most peculiar and interesting part of the Queen Bee is the *ovaries*, or egg-bag. It consists of a pair of organs, represented by FF in the cut. Each is composed of tubes full of eggs, in every stage of growth which start from near the apex H and open into one duct on each side as shown in the cut. Each egg passes through a common channel C on its way to the cell, passing by a little sac I, called the "spermatheca," from which all eggs destined to become workers are impregnated in passing.

The body and legs of bees are covered with fine hairs, to which pollen

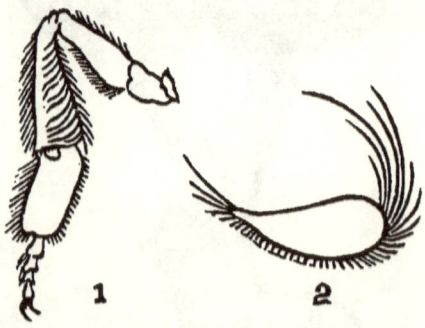

adheres, which is brushed off by the bee and packed in baskets on their hind legs.

A young queen seems incapable of fertilization after she is three weeks old, and lays only drone eggs. She is generally fertilized at from five to twelve days of age; in which act, this sac I is filled with seminal fluid from the drone. It is now generally believed that the queen is able to fertilize the eggs as they pass the spermatheca, at her option. Adjacent organs are represented by the letters A B D and E.

We would recommend every beginner to transfer his bees at once when the fruit blossoms appear, in to hives with movable combs, so that he may use intelligent judgment on the subject. (See transferring.) This operation seems at first formidable, but if the bees are well smoked, (see smoker,) they will soon fill themselves with honey, and be almost as harmless as flies, unless mashed. If no smoker is at hand a roll of coarse cotton cloth may be used for the purpose. Place it well lighted under the mouth of the hive, and the bees will soon be subdued. The peculiar sound which they set up indicates subjugation. In movable comb hives, we speak of the l)wer box as the *broodnest*, and the upper one as the *cap*, or *upper chamber*.

As to hives, adopt some good pattern, and stick to it. Make them so exact that every part of each will fit with that part of another. This is very important for many advantages are gained in an apiary by the interchange of frames and parts of hives. For entrances, we recommend only one in front, three-eighths by three inches, which can be supplemented by auger holes above. These can be stopped with corks for winter.

Every hive should have at least one closely fitting divison board in order to contract the space for the colony according to its strength and the season.

Do not be afraid of feeding bees when no honey is gathered in the fields. If done regularly and systematically it will often repay one hundred fold. (See "Feeding," page 112).

Always aim to keep *strong colonies*. These are always the best in every respect, except at times when a number of queens are to be reared. Then *nucleus*, or small hives may be used. (See "Queen Rearing.") Strong stocks will be most apt to rear bright Italian queens, but if the weather is cold queens are more apt to be dark colored. In handling queens never catch them by the body, but by the wing. In searching in the hive for the queen she is most apt to be found on combs from which young bees are just hatching. It is best to open hives in the warm part of the day, both because then the propolis is soft and the combs are not necessarily jarred in removing them, and because then most of the old bees are absent in the fields.

In opening a hive blow smoke into the entrance for a few moments, until the subdued hum is distinctly heard, and as the quilt is lifted from one corner, follow it up with smoke. Stand on the side towards which the wind is blowing, least your breath madden the bees. Remember that the human breath is very offensive to them, and do not breathe directly on them, or you may suffer thereby.

We recommend beginners always to use a bee veil to to protect the face, and if fearful, also at first, rubber gloves or coarse yarn ones. Gloves of buckskin, leather, and kid have proved of little value, as bees easily sting through them. It is well to have an extra veil or two on hand for use by a visiting friend. As one becomes accustomed to the work he can by degrees leave these off as he finds himself able. But we would caution against entering hives carelessly, because they have been very gentle. Sometimes when the honey ceases to flow, a colony heretofore the most peaceable, will sting severely if opened without proper precaution.

Let no *patent* man beguile you into using moth traps. Strong colonies are the best preventives against their depredations. The presence of an unfertile or drone-laying queen, or a fertile worker may be suspected by eggs irregularly laid or found dropped about, outside the cells.

When honey is scarce in the fields, be careful to leave no sweets exposed, and if robbing commences, be quick to stop it, before great mischief is done. (See "Robbing," page 101).

A word of caution is always necessary to the beginner, least he overdo the matter of increasing his stocks. Remember the bee-keeper is rich, not according to the number, but according to the strength of his colonies during the honey season. Never attempt to do more than double your bees if honey is desired, and unless the season is specially good do not make more than one new swarm from two colonies.

If an Italian queen is reared for introduction, and you wish to catch her for any purpose, let her fly upon the window, when she can be readily caught by the wing. Decide on the manner of introducing her to the colony to be used,(See "Introducing Queens," p. 110) and do it as gently as possible. Release the queen when the hive is as quiet as possible:

Beginners sometimes think that it is too expensive to paint hives. This is a mistake. One cannot afford *not* to paint them, because they will soon injure in exposure to the weather by splitting, swelling, or warping, so as to fit badly, and cause much greater loss than the cost of painting. We prefer three good coats, all white or clouded, though the paints should be of different colors, to be distinguished by the bees. Dark colored hives become much hotter in summer by absorbing the rays of the sun, and the new comb is much more liable to melt down than in white hives.

Less expense attends providing proper hives for bees, according to the income derived from them, than any stock about the farm. Stables, barns, sheds, daries, cow-houses, &c., are necessary for stock, which do not yield proportionally better returns than bees, in the management of which, even on a large scale, all that is necessary, are hives—which are of permanent value—a wax extractor, and a honey extractor. Yearly there will be need for comb-foundation, frames, boxes, and crates, or jars. But these last cost no more than what is oftentimes necessary for properly marketing some other things. Besides this, a good honey house is necessary, if there is no building at hand to be used for such.

Perhaps a more specific description of these later improvements, and the advantages of their use, may be of value to beginners: Brood comb seems to be the foundation of development in a hive. Its presence is necessary to a proper conduct of the business of the hive. If not present, bees must make it before rapid normal development in the hive is possible. Honey-comb is made entirely of pure wax. This is a secretion from the body of the bee, [see page 47]. In order to build this comb, they must consume some fifteen or twenty times its weight in honey, besides the time necessary for the wax secretion. The importance of giving to bees, combs ready made, has long been known. They will unite and use any scraps of comb which may be preserved and fastened temporarily into frames. Nice pieces of drone comb may advantageously be used in honey boxes. But the difficulty of getting a supply of natural comb, led to various experiments in order to supply, artificially this deficiency. During the last year these sheets of artificial comb-foundation were largely used, and firmly established as of very great utility in the apiary.

Until recently, attempts at making artificial comb, both in Germany and England, were from the use of plates, which were necessarily slow. But more recently, machines have been made by which continuous sheets of wax, of proper thickness, are, on passing between its engraved rollers, impressed on both sides with the exact bottoms of cells as made by the bees, and between each, a shoulder of wax is left which the bees quickly lengthen into side walls. The demand for this article, says one of the largest manufacturers of it, "Is increasing so steadily, that it is quite probable the supply of wax will be the only limit to its manufacture and use."

It is important that *pure wax* should be used, for all substitutes proposed for it have heretofore failed.

The wax sheets are made by dipping a sheet of galvanized iron into a vessel of melted wax. By dipping two or three times, according to the temperature of the heated wax, the sheets will be of sufficient thickness. The wax is scaled from the sheets and when well cooled, rolled through the foundation machine. Soap suds rubbed upon the rolls will prevent the sheets from sticking, but as bees seem sometimes to object to it, water into which a little bark, called *soap bark* is put, is now generally used, and seems to answer as well. We are, by the advice of A. I. Root, now using, with great satisfaction, common starch, prepared as for starching clothes. The roller should be well wet with it before use, and when necessary.

These sheets are readily cut up into smaller pieces of any desired dimensions. Perhaps the best way to cut them, where many are used, is with a cutter made from a round piece of tin, filed sharp on the circumference and fixed to run as a wheel on a pivot through the centre, which fastens it to the handle. This can be run rapidly along any guide to mark the size required.

HOW TO FASTEN COMB-FOUNDATION IN FRAMES.

This is done in different ways. It is important that it be *fastened firmly all along the top bar*, in order to prevent sagging. Some use melted wax or white glue, but they are troublesome, and when used in honey boxes are apt to leave a lump of the substance on the bar, which is decidedly objectionable.

We recommend fastening them by placing the frames bottom upwards on a table, and laying the sheet on the top bar so that the edge comes nearly across it. Now, take a screw driver or piece of smooth firm iron, and rub it down hard to the wood until it adheres all along. One corner of the iron should go entirely to the wood at the finishing stroke. On this tack a small thin strip of wood into the top bar, so placed that when the sheet is bent up against it, it hangs in the centre of the frame. If the frames have comb guides, the comb is fastened to in it the same manner, but there is not always need for the extra strip to be tacked on. When frames are filled with foundation, they should be hung in an empty hive or similar box so as to be preserved from injury until needed. The best way we have seen for fastening comb into the small honey boxes or sections, is to make a small groove or saw cut in the centre of the upper bar and fasten it in by bending it open or by sticking it in whilst warm with wax or glue.

There are many advantages gained by the use of comb-foundation, some of which we will enumerate:

First. In transferring bees if every other frame be filled with it they will all be filled with straight combs.

Second. When bees are inclined to build too much drone comb, the hive is easily filled with worker comb by its use.

Third. In early Spring it is very valuable to insert in the broodnest, to stimulate breeding, and assist in rapidly building up the colony or in forming new ones, which otherwise would be checked from the lack of comb.

Fourth. To insert in a choice hive to secure eggs for queen rearing, on a new soft comb on which bees are most apt to build good queen-cells.

Fifth To have on hand in extracting, to insert in one or two of the first hives opened, in order to get a supply of combs ahead, so as not to open a hive but once.

Sixth. To insert when full combs of dark honey are set away for wintering.

Seventh. To prevent too much drone rearing.

Eighth. To give the queen extra room at any time in manipulating a hive when it is not just convenient to extract at the time.

Ninth. To secure continuous breeding by feeding, at times when combs are scarce or when bees are loth to build.

Tenth. To gather full supplies of fall honey at a time when bees are not inclined to to build comb.

Eleventh. To insure at any time straight comb, for easy management.

Twelfth. To stimulate bees to work quickly in boxes. It is doubtful whether it is advisable to use much of it in the boxes; though practiced largely by some, yet a small strip does induce them to work more quickly in the boxes.

It is extremely important that only *pure bees-wax* be used, and especially is this the case if any is to be used as the foundation of box honey for the table.

This shows the importance of using the Wax Extractor, spoken of on page 53, by which alone pure wax can be obtained. This wax should be carefully saved by every apiarian in a shape suitable to be made into comb foundation, as above described. Those who have the machines advertise to give one pound of foundation for two of *pure wax*. This exchange is far better for small apiarians, than for them to attempt to make it for themselves. We advise all to avail themselves of the great advantages of comb-foundation, and also of the honey extractor.

As many beginners do not understand the principle on which the extractor works, nor the advantages gained by its use, we will here more minutely describe its mechanism, mode of use, and advantages gained by it.

It is sometimes called the *honey slinger*, because when operated the honey is thrown or *slung* from the cells by centrifugal force, and drawn off at the bottom into a receiving vessel. There are various kinds of good extractors in the market, some one of which every apiarian should have. They all act on the centrifugal princple, and consist of a can to catch the honey, and a revolving wire cloth basket within, which receives the comb and turns with it. This should be run with a gearing above. A temporary one might be made with ingenuity, from a large barrel, after painting it well with wax, but good tin ones are now so cheap that it is best and cheapest in the end, to buy one of these. The can should have a faucet near the bottom for drawing off the honey.

The size of the frame used, regulates both the size of basket and the can. The basket should be of light material built on a shaft which turns in a nut at the bottom, by means of a single gearing at the top Two opposite sides of the basket should be made of tinned wire cloth, supported by strips of tin and a little larger than the frames to be used. The wire cloth against which the combs lie in extracting, should be *tinned*, and not merely galvanized, for the acids in honey will corrode the galvanized iron and poison it to some extent. It should have from three and a half to five meshes to the inch. The basket should be two or three inches from the bottom to give some space for honey below and as much above to prevent it from spraying over the top. The cylinder is made of good tin, with heavy wire in the top to strengthen it. The bottom is made of a round piece of tin, a little larger than the space to be filled by it. From one side cut out a trangular section to the centre or a little beyond, and in its place sodder a similar piece a little larger, and previously bent in to the shape of a trough. The bottom, thus fixed will permit all the honey to run towards the centre and then down the trough through the faucet. There is fastened on and over this, a tin hoop, four or five inches wide, made stiff with wire on the bottom edge, soldered on for it to rest upon. No covering is needed when in use, but to keep out insects, at other times, any kind of a simple covering will answer, though perhaps none is more convenient than a circular piece of cloth of proper size with a rubber cord in the hem. When honey is gathered plentifully, any convenient shady place answers well for extracting, but if scarce, the combs must be carried into some house out of the way of the bees. Sometimes it is more convenient to use for this purpose, a movable tent, covered with cotton cloth. If so, it is easily made from scantling for the bottom, and poles which support the cloth fastened in auger holes. They are easily lifted from the holes and folded away when desirable.

A little experience will teach one, how fast and long to turn, to extract the honey. Open the hive gently, after smoking the bees for a moment. Shake the bees directly on the top of the frames or on a board in front. In the first method there is less danger of losing the queen or of inducing robbing. Brush the bees off with a tuft of broomcorn or a green twig. A feather is not so good; it seems to irritate the bees. Place the comb gently in the extractor, and turn very gently if the comb is new or the frame not filled. If very heavy with honey do not aim to get it all from the first side, until it has been turned, because heavy new comb is injured by the wires mashing into it, when the velocity is great.

ADVANTAGES OF THE EXTRACTOR.

We caution against a too free use of the extractor, unless prepared to feed if necessary, should a honey drought come when stores are thus too much reduced, or if done too late in the fall.

Judiciously used, the extractor is of great advantage in the following points, as given by Rev. J. W. Shearer in THE BEE-KEEPERS' MAGAZINE, Vol. V., No. 6, page 115:

"First. In a good honey harvest, the cells of hatching brood are afterwards filled with honey, so that the queen has little room to rear brood. When this is the case, the bees will decrease very rapidly, and are sometimes lost. Extracting the honey gives the queen room, stimulates the workers, strengthens the swarm, and helps to keep it in good condition to take advantage of the next honey harvest.

"Second. Bees will often lay up honey rapidly in combs furnished by extracting, when they will not make new combs.

"Third. This is true, especially in the fall harvest, when instinct prompts them to store honey rapidly, when there is but little in the hive. Seldom is more rapid work seen than in a spring colony closely extracted in the fall. Each bee seems to be racing with his neighbor. Instinct prompts to build but little comb in the fall, and it is often too cool for box building some time before they cease to lay up in the hive. Hence, much less fall honey is obtained, when box honey alone is relied on. The full benefit of fall extracting, is gotten only when the apiarian has experience and expertness in rapidly supplying syrup for wintering. Without this, a fear of losing the bees should check a too free use of the extractor.

"Fourth. When the extractor is mainly relied on, after a hive has been swarmed, it may be doubled in this way: giving a great deal of comb and a quantity of bees. Swarm a stand by the exchange method, and instead of placing the old stock containing the young workers and brood on a new stand, place them in the second story of this stock. Thus a double set of comb is given, the hive, full of comb, is soon full of bees by the hatching above and below; has a fertile queen below, which is necessarily prolific, whilst much honey is stored above for extracting.

"By this method, instead of increasing by swarming in the summer, strong colonies have the swarming propensity gratified, and are kept at work. By raising queens in August and setting away full combs, they are easily separated into good strong colonies for winter. Extracted honey may be put directly into barrels or cans. In this case it is much more apt to candy. After ripening or evaporating for a few days it is less liable to candy. It is a great trouble thus to preserve it, since all insects will drop into it and get drowned. The best mode of taking care of extracted honey is to put it directly into fruit cans, and seal up when almost at the boiling point. Thus the air is driven out and it seldom candies. It may be heated in large quantities and at once put up securely, so that there is no loss from leakage, or a second handling, or any fear of impurities from insects or dust. It is then ready for market. The cans are useful in every household when the honey is used up, and the consumer does not feel that he is paying for useless bottles."

The value of these great improvements in apiculture are so well acknowledged, that it is hardly necessary to add any testimonials. Leading apiarians everywhere agree concerning the advantages of the extractor, and of comb-foundation for the broodnest. Some yet argue against its use in boxes, on the ground of impurities in the wax, which may endanger the price of box honey. The Bellows Smoker is one of these simple conveniences, concerning which the testimony constantly received is: "I could not do without it." "I would not take $50 or $100 for mine, if it could not be replaced." "It is more than is claimed for it," &c. Every beginner should furnish himself with a veil, a bellows smoker, and—even though not over two hives are kept—an extractor will pay the first year.

GOLDEN RULES.

FIRST.—Keep all colonies strong. This is the best protection against moths and robbers; the surest way to secure an abundance of surplus honey, and such colonies, with sufficient stores, are wintered most safely.

SECOND.—In handling bees, be *gentle*. Subdue them, if necessary, with smoke, which causes them to fill themselves with honey. "A bee filled with liquid sweets, will not volunteer an attack." If stung, *scrape* off the sting at once.

THIRD.—Have the hive carefully protected from the severe and sudden changes in spring.

FOURTH.—*Hives*—Let all hives and parts of hives be interchangeable

FIFTH.—*Swarming*—Have queen-cells or young queens ready before dividing. These are most conveniently raised with regular sized frames.

SIXTH.—*Inserting Queens*—Let the colony be conscious of its loss, destroy all queen-cells, let the same scent be given, and the bees be as quiet as possible when the operation is performed.

SEVENTH.—Secure and pack honey in attractive packages, easily handled.

EIGHTH.—Judicious feeding, systematically followed in times of drought, pays well.

HOW TO REMOVE HONEY BOXES AND EXPEL THE BEES.

Near sunset remove the cap and raise the end of the box just enough to blow under a little smoke, when the bees will leave the holes, which may be covered with blocks or an empty box turned bottom up. Set the full boxes right side up on strips upon the stand, so that they shall be three eights of an inch from the board and five or six inches from the entrance of the hive. Gently rap upon the boxes until the bees begin in good earnest to leave for the hive. Being filled with honey there is no danger of their stinging from the rough treatment received. The humming of those that enter will give notice to the others of their position near their home. Should some remain in the boxes they may be left till morning if the weather be pleasant, but must be removed early, least the bees commence carrying the honey into the hive. If preferred the boxes may be placed upon their sides in a tight box or barrel, and a thin cloth thrown over the top. Seeing the light the bees will creep up on the cloth, and if this be turned over occasionally all except a few young ones will find their way back to the hive. Late in the season, when the nights are cool, if this cap be raised in the evening, the boxes will usually be clear of bees by morning. As soon as the flowers have failed or the bees commence carrying down honey from the unsealed cells, all boxes should be removed, unless, as is sometimes the case, when the latter part of the season has been unfavorable, an insufficient supply has been stored in the body of the hive. In this case if not left, the bees should be fed. (See "Feeding," page 148.)

CHAPTER V.

ARTIFICIAL SWARMING.

THAT bees may be swarmed artificially, although not known to all even at the present day, is not a late discovery, but has been practiced for over a century, with more or less success, depending entirely upon the observance of the three following conditions, to wit: the *proper time* for swarming; the condition of the stock; and whether the method employed was in harmony with or in violation of the laws which govern the economy of the hive.

1st. The time for swarming is not until the yield of honey is abundant and drones are numerous in the apiary, nor should it be performed so late in the season that the bees will not have time to become strong in numbers and rich in stores before the frosts of autumn cut short the pasturage. The safest rule, for the inexperienced, is to wait until natural swarms begin to issue, *unless* he can have a finished queen-cell to give the queenless part, or, what is much better, a fertile queen, in which case he may swarm somewhat earlier or later than the usual time for natural swarms.

2d. The stock to be swarmed should be very populous, for if swarmed when too weak, it is thus robbed of its power to generate heat for breeding, and should unfavorable weather ensue both parts will often be deficient in numbers and stores for winter; whereas, had the stock been left until it could have spared a swarm, both would be prepared for winter, beside yielding ample returns in surplus honey as the reward of proper management. There will sometimes be a season when these conditions will not occur in all the stocks in the apiary. Such stocks should not be swarmed that season. *The only safeguard against poor seasons is* STRONG STOCKS, for they will work while others are idle.

3d. The value of any method depends, in a great measure upon the certainty of, and the time required for, supplying the queenless part with a *fertile* queen. Yet, the method any one should adopt, or whether he should allow his bees to swarm *once* naturally, will depend much upon his desire for increase of stocks, and the number of colonies or apiaries he may wish to manage. Hence, we shall describe several methods, contrasting their advantages and disadvantages with natural swarming. The practice of multiplying colonies by artificial means, has the following advantages over natural swarming:

1st. The trouble and risk of swarms issuing when the bee-keeper is absent, or several issuing about the same time and clustering together or leaving for the woods, is avoided.

2d. As soon as the stocks are in proper condition they may all be swarmed when most convenient and you are certain of the increase; but in natural swarming, only a *few days* of bad weather will frequently cause the queen cells to be destroyed and swarming to be postponed for weeks and often till the next season.

HOW TO MAKE SWARMS BY DIVIDING."

We will give the principal methods for swarming bees in the movable-comb hive, any one of which may be used according to circumstances or the choice of the bee-keeper. The following process is the most convenient when making swarms away from home. Spread a sheet upon the ground, and after blowing a little smoke into the entrance of the hive raise it carefully and place it upon the sheet. If it is taken any distance from the old stand, an empty hive should be left, to hold the returning bees. Also place upon the edge of the sheet your new hive, with the cap and frames removed, entrance closed and movable side in. Proceed to open the old hive; meanwhile quieting the bees with your smoke. Separate the young bees from the old ones by shaking them from the combs upon the sheet three feet or more in front of the hive. When shaking a comb, hold it perpendicular, to prevent breaking, and dislodge the bees with a downward shake. If the weather be warm and the combs new and tender, instead of shaking them brush off the bees with a wing or quill. Keep a sharp watch for the queen by running the eye over each comb, both before and after shaking it.

Do not spend much time, however, in looking for the queen, except to be careful not to put her into the hive which is to contain most of the combs. As fast as the combs are shaken, set them into the new hive. If the queen be found, place the comb upon which she rests and another comb containing honey in one of the hives with one-fourth of the bees, and give the balance of the combs and three-fourths of the bees to the other hive. Fill the vacancies in both hives with the empty frames, and place the one with the queen and two combs upon the old stand, as enough bees will return to it from the one on the new stand to make the colonies about equal. But if the queen is not found while shaking off the bees, place the two combs (one of them containing eggs and young larvæ) in the old hive and put in the empty frames. By this time most of the old bees will probably have entered. When there are but three or four quarts left upon the sheet, place the old hive upon its own stand and let the young bees enter the new hive by making them travel, thinly, a considerable distance over the sheet, that you may find the queen, should she happen to be among them, and return her to the old hive. Contract the entrance of the new hive, which may now be placed in any desired location.

Another way of making new swarms where there are several stocks in movable-comb hives, is to select four stocks and take two combs from each. Brush back all the bees into their own hives, that no stock be robbed of its queen. Fill the vacancies in each hive with empty frames, placing them near the centre, where they will be quickly filled. Place the removed combs together in an empty hive. Remove a strong stock (in any kind of hive) when the bees are flying briskly, and place the hive containing the combs on its stand. If the strong stock were taken a rod or two away, near the middle of the day in good honey gathering weather, enough bees will return to the old stand to make the swarm. Contract the entrance to both hives for a day or two. This method has some advantages, for as each old stock loses but one or two combs at a time, a new swarm can be made from every five stocks as often as the loss is regained, and yet all the stocks, both old and new, be in condition for winter, should swarming be continued past the usual season. Whenever the weather becomes unfavorable, or pasturage seems to be failing, swarming should be discontinued till honey is again plenty.

Another method, is to take out half the combs with the bees adhering to them, and place them in the new hive; put in the empty frames, and set the hives a foot or two apart, one on the right and the other on the left of the old stand. They must be watched an hour or two, to keep the bees about equal. If one hive seems to be getting more than its share, move that a little farther from, or the other nearer to, the old stand. A board set up between them and projecting a little in front will help divide the returning bees. If the hives are not the same color, the old one must be partially covered with a cloth, to change its appearance, else it will get most of the bees. If the queenless part be not determined by the motion of the bees, it may be known in two or three days by its having started queen-cells.

If a fertile queen is not at hand for the queenless part, prevent the construction of much drone comb by giving it all but one or two of the combs. In taking them from the other hive, brush back all the bees, lest the queen be removed. If more stocks be divided in eight or ten days, a queen-cell for each queenless part may be obtained from this stock.

The queenless part of a divided stock should have the date of its division marked upon the hive or otherwise noted, for if a queen-cell was not inserted at the time of dividing, it will have its queen-cells finished by the tenth or eleventh day, when all but one should be destroyed or used for dividing other stocks. If this is not attended to, a colony will often injure itself by swarming, although it may have but two or three quarts of bees. All colonies raising queens should be carefully examined in about twenty-five days from the time of dividing, or if finished queen-cells were given them, in fifteen days, to see that they have a fertile queen, and if no eggs can be found in the combs the presumption is that some accident has happened the queen. If a nucleus, containing a fertile queen is at hand, introduce her. If neither queen nor queen-cell can be had, give the colony a comb of brood and eggs taken from a hive that has a fertile queen. This will not only enable them to rear a queen, but the maturing brood will materially strengthen the swarm. When dividing, care must be taken in all cases to place the combs containing brood or eggs, compactly together, that the bees may be able to cover them and prevent chilling the brood. By inserting a frame or two of empty comb in each new colony, the brood may be enclosed in smaller space and the heat economized. Queenless or removed colonies should have their entrances contracted for a few days to exclude both the cool air and inquisitive robber bees. In all these methods, as in natural swarming, we are liable to have queenless colonies by the loss of young queens, when making their excursions to meet the drones. Beside, a colony will do little while rearing a queen, which consumes much time, usually in the height of honey gathering. Hence, perfection will not be reached short of introducing a fertile queen at the time of swarming.

THE NUCLEUS SYSTEM OF SWARMING.

"*The introduction of a mature fertile queen to a colony two weeks sooner than when they swarm naturally, is an advantage sufficient to pay for extra trouble. The time gained in breeding is equivalent to a swarm.*"—M. QUINBY.

In swarming bees on this system, we first rear a queen in a small cluster—nucleus—of bees, allowing the nucleus hive to remain in its place until the queen becomes fertile, when we swarm the bees by simply causing the two hives to exchange places. Unlike natural swarming, the old queen remains in the parent stock, and its labors go on scarcely interrupted. The system is based upon the well known law, that bees, after luxuriating upon the flowers, will return to the exact spot of their old habitation.

Form a nucleus from an Italian or other populous stock by blowing a few whiffs of smoke into the entrance, and opening the hive, select a frame of comb containing capped brood, but especialy plenty of eggs and young larvæ. After looking this over carefully, lest the old queen be removed, place it with its adhering bees in the empty hive, and next to it another comb containing honey, which will afford protection to the brood and food for the bees. As many of the old bees will return to the parent stock, give the nucleus hive at least a quart of bees and set it on a new stand two or three rods distant. Contract the entrance so that but one or two bees can pass at the same time, and set a feed pan on the frames, or a sponge filled with sweetened water will supply their wants until the young bees go to work in their new location. In place of the combs removed from the parent stock, set in empty frames with a full one between. If the frames are put near the centre, the old stock will increase all the faster, as the queen will fill the new comb with eggs as fast as it is built. The removal of the two combs stimulates the bees to great activity by giving them room to work, and detaches just bees enough to prevent their clustering idly about the entrance. The nucleus will construct queen-cells and rear a queen as well as a whole swarm. Beside, the queen is easily found among so few bees. We now wait until the tenth or eleventh day, from the time the nucleus was formed, when we open it, and, with a sharp thin bladed pocket-knife, cut out all the queen cells *but one*, and use them immediately in forming other nuclei, by attaching one of them to a frame of comb and bees taken from an old stock, as before described, and placed in an empty hive. In transferring queen-cells great care must be taken not to press or dent them, or expose them long to the hot sun or cool air for fear of destroying the royal occupants. The beginner should remove but one at a time, returning the frame from which it is taken to its place in the hive until the royal cell is adjusted in its new location. When practicable, leave about an inch square of comb attached to the cell, and upon taking the comb of brood from the old stock, make an opening among the eggs and

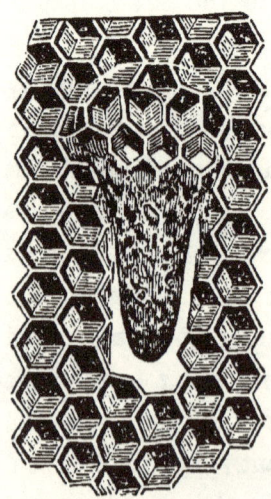

12. Queen-cell Inserted.

larvæ where the bees will be sure to cluster upon it and keep it warm, and carefully insert it as shown in figure 12, leaving an open space below it.

If the first nucleus was formed from the only Italian stock in the yard, and more queen-cells are wanted, remove every queen-cell from it, and add another comb of eggs and brood from its parent stock. But when no more queen-cells are needed, leave one to hatch, and as by this time the brood will all be capped over, the bees will be liable to follow the young queen on her excursion to meet the drones. To prevent this, exchange one of the combs for one containing eggs and young larvæ, when forming the other nuclei. Young queens will return unless lost by birds or other casualties, to which *all* queens are *once* exposed. Such loss is easily ascertained among so few bees, and we have only to insert another queen-cell, adding a comb containing eggs and brood, and repeat the trial. Should the parent stock be very populous, it may be swarmed by taking a queen from a nucleus belonging to a less populous stock, and another queen reared there.

WHEN AND HOW TO SWARM THE BEES.

Every populous stock, from which a nucleus has been formed, should be swarmed, if the weather is favorable, as soon as the queen in the nucleus has become fertile. This is, usually, in from six to ten days after inserting the queen-cell, and is readily determined by examining the combs for eggs. We now, unless the yield of honey is very abundant, confine the young queen in a gauze wire cage. Having filled up the nucleus hive with empty frames, exchange the places of the two hives, bringing the entrance of the nucleus hive where the old stock has stood, and where the mass of the old bees will return from the fields, thus throwing out of the old stock swarms of workers into the nucleus hive, while the old bees from the nucleus will enter the old hive and minister to the wants of the numerous brood of the parent stock. The bees *must not* be swarmed between the hatching and fertilization of the queen, and should they be swarmed when the honey harvest has received a check from a storm or drought, the bees thus empty of honey and consequently more quarrelsome, being suddenly thrown into the presence of a strange queen (although of the same scent) are inclined to sting her. To prevent this she is caged for thirty-six hours, when the bees from the old stock will mostly have joined the nucleus colony and she may be safely liberated. But, if she was taken from another nucleus, we sometimes let her remain caged a day longer, or smear her well with warm honey and drop her in among the bees. They immediately commence licking up the honey and *forget* to sting her.

If from any cause the stocks are swarmed when the bees are working but little, and after three or four days the nucleus swarm be found deficient in bees, it may be strengthened by exchanging some of its empty frames for frames of capped brood from the parent stock, or should the flowers yield bountifully within a week, the location of the two hives may again be exchanged. The bees will not quarrel as they are of the same scent, unless a nucleus has been formed several weeks, or when honey is scarce, it is sometimes necessary to treat both stocks—especially the old one—to tobacco smoke. This precaution, however, is only for the inexperienced, since, in the midst of the swarming season, when the flowers are yielding in profusion, little protection is needed either for the queen or the operator.

ADVANTAGES OF THE NUCLEUS SYSTEM.

The superiority of this system may be seen by contrasting it with any other method of swarming. Unlike natural swarming, by this system all our new swarms have young queens, and as drone comb is seldom built during the first year of the queen's existence, we get the frames filled almost exclusively with worker comb. By it our stocks and colonies are never without fertile queens. Hence, breeding and honey gathering go on as before, keeping all our swarms strong and safe against moths and other enemies. But in natural swarming (which, if properly managed in movable-comb hives, is preferable to most methods) much time is consumed in idleness by the whole swarm rearing a queen in the best part of the season, besides honey gathering is nearly suspended for ten days after the issue of the first swarm, and no eggs are laid for from two to three weeks, or until the fertilization of the young queen, and before these mature, so great is the mortality of bees at this season that the stock is sometimes lost from lack of bees to protect its combs. While, had it been supplied with a fertile queen, it could soon have spared another swarm—so incredibly fast do bees breed during the honey harvest. If by the introduction of a fertile queen, " the time gained in breeding is equivalent to a swarm," (and we think no close observer will doubt it,) then it follows that we could swarm a stock twice on the nucleus system with no more risk than swarming once naturally, or that we are as safe against poor seasons as those who increase on an average but one-half annually. Yet as "safety and certainty" is our motto, we recommend only doubling the number of populous stocks, at which rate ten stocks would increase to one hundred and sixty in four years if every stock was swarmed annually, which number may be made good, and even a more rapid increase safely secured by using the surplus honey stored in frames, as directed under "how to stock an apiary." In short, by the nucleus system of swarming, the vexatious losses attending other methods are avoided, and the process is so easy and gradual that even the day-laborer or business man, when supplied with hives, will find leisure time enough to manage quite a number of stocks with profit and pleasure. Whilst bees might be managed successfully by doubling each year, more honey can be obtained by keeping the stocks all very strong, and only making one swarm from two hives. By the use of artificial comb-foundation, great advantage is gained. Swarms may be built up much more rapidly by giving sheets of this, and not waiting for combs to be built before the queen can lay eggs. Some bee-keepers have been very successful in rapidly increasing stocks, and each year establishing new apiaries by putting the extra hives out on shares to new parties. The owner generally furnishes hives, bees, boxes, and owns all the increase. The other does the work and in the fall the surplus honey is divided equally.

CHAPTER V.

ITALIAN BEES.

This variety of the honey bee, called also Ligurian bee, is found in small districts amid the Alps, embracing portions of Switzerland and Northern Italy. They are of a striped golden color, and were described by Aristotle, Virgil, and other ancient writers, as variegated in color, and the most valuable kind then known, but for centuries they were unknown outside of the districts above named, the surrounding mountains covered with perpetual snow being impassable by their wings.

They were accidentally discovered, during the wars of Napoleon, by Captain Baldenstein, who carried the first colony across the Alps in 1843. In 1853 they were introduced by Dzierzon into Germany, and into the United States in 1860. There has since been several importations. We were slow to believe all the good things said of them by German apiarians, until convinced of their superiority by the universal testimony of prominent American bee-keepers, coupled with our own experience. We present a few extracts.

"We believe that the superiority of the Italian bee is no longer questionable."—*California Culturist.*

"All agreed as to the superiority of the Italian to the common black bee."—*From the Report of the American Apiarian Convention.*

At the Wisconsin Bee-keepers' Convention, in February, 1866, the following resolution was passed unanimously:

"*Resolved,* That the Italian (or Ligurian) bee, fully sustains its European reputation, and this association heartily recommend it for general cultivation, as being more hardy, vigorous, and fertile, and, as a consequence, more profitable."

" Of their superiority there can be no question."—*Dr. Metcalf.*

Dr. Kirtland, of Cleveland, Ohio, says: "My colonies are daily watched and admired by many visitors. So far as my experience has gone, I find every statement in regard to their superiority sustained. They will no doubt prove a valuable acquisition to localities of high altitude, and will be peculiarly adapted to the climate of Washington Territory, Oregon, and the mountainous regions of California."

Mr. Langstroth says: " If we may judge from the working of my colonies, the Italians will fully sustain their European reputation. They have gathered more than twice as much honey as the swarms of the common bee. This honey has been chiefly gathered within the last few weeks, during which time the swarms of common bees have increased in weight but very little. The season here has been eminently unfavorable for the new swarms —one of the worst I ever knew—and the prospect now is, that I shall have to feed all of them except the Italians."

"The great German apiarian, Mr. Dzierzon, informs us that his apiaries, (now consisting of more than six hundred colonies,) having been thoroughly *Italianized* in 1858, produced him last year (1859) more than double the quantity of honey ever ob tained by him in any previous year. The season there was very favorable, and in the fall there was an unusual abundance of buckwheat pasturage in his neighborhood."—*Ed. American Bee Journal.*

Mrs. E. S. Tupper, of Brighton, Iowa, a noted Western writer on bee culture, says: "In the summer of 1863 I had but two Italian stocks to commence with. One of these stored one hundred and ten pounds of honey, besides giving me three artificial swarms; the other gave me two swarms and stored ninety-six pounds of honey; and all the swarms but one, partly filled several boxes each. I had, that same season, fifty-six colonies of common bees, all of which were divided, but not one of which stored a pound of honey, though in the same kind of hives and treated in a similar way with the Italians. That season it will be remembered was very poor.

"In the summer of 1864, I averaged from nine Italian colonies one hundred and nineteen pounds each. The greatest yield from one hive was as follows: one full swarm taken from it the fifteenth of May; honey taken in boxes through the season, one hundred and fifty-six pounds, besides four full frames from which to rear queens; the swarm from it stored eighty pounds in a cap, and on the fifteenth of July threw off a very large swarm, which filled its hive, and stored several pounds in boxes. Thus we have two hundred and thirty-six pounds of box honey, besides two extra large colonies, from a single hive, not reckoning the frames and partially filled boxes. I do not think a colony of the common bee ever did as much in the best season; if so, let us have the record."

Having now had an experience of several years with Italian bees, spending much of our time in the apiary, rearing queens, we find them to possess the following points of superiority over the common black bee:

Their individual strength being greater, they fly with less fatigue and are more active and successful in defending their stores against both the moth-miller and robber bees. They gather honey—especially when other sources fail—from iron weed, thistle and other flowers which are seldom visited by the black bees, working quite freely upon the seed crop of red clover, when other late forage is cut short by drought. They also work more steadily during the season, even when there is but little honey to be gathered from any source, and it being a well known fact that breeding keeps pace with honey gathering, the result is, strong stocks, which secure a large product of honey, and are proof against the moth-worm and poor seasons. Hence the importance of the above peculiarities cannot easily be over estimated, and they account in part for the following characteristic differences between the two races of bees:

1st. The Italian queens are called "prolific breeders," as the stocks breed earlier in the season and continue later, casting larger swarms and swarming on an average about two weeks earlier than the black bee, thereby gaining that much time in the best of the gathering season, and usually swarming in seasons when common bees do not.

2d. They gather much larger stores of honey than the black bees, as proven by the united testimony of eminent apiarians both in Europe and America.

POINTS OF SUPERIORITY. 111

3d. In opening a hive, the Italians, when *pure*, are much more peaceable than the black bees, and the queen is more readily found, not so much on account of contrast in color as from the fact that with the workers she usually remains undisturbed upon the combs.

4th. Being more constant workers, the Italians are less inclined to rob than the native bees. Being hardier, they are longer lived, winter more safely, and are more inclined to supercede their queens when past their prime. Hence, colonies are not so liable to become queenless, and queenless stocks do not so rapidly become depopulated.

5th. Their beauty of color and graceful form render them an object of interest to every person of taste. Hence, they attract many visitors, who admire the golden hues, so beautifully shown by the sun's rays, as they pass swiftly to and from the hive.

IMPORTANCE OF NEW BLOOD IN THE APIARY.

Whilst we fully endorse the great benefits resulting from the introduction of Italian bees, we doubt after years' of experience and observation whether the benefits result so much from the superiority of the Italian bee itself, as from the admixture of foreign blood, thereby correcting, to a great extent the mischief that has resulted from too long *in and in breeding*. And this benefit has been due directly to the supposed, and claimed, supericrity of the Italian bee, to obtain, which extra efforts were put forth. Many of our closest observing apiarists are beginning to doubt whether Italians are really so much preferable to hybrids, as is sometimes claimed.

We are inclined to believe that there is great truth in the statements of Rev. J. W. Shearer, in our "BEE-KEEPERS MAGAZINE," of January last, from which we make some quotations:

" Every farmer is well aware of the injury resulting from too close breeding for successive generations among his horses, cattle or fowls; but no attention, or but little, was paid to this by bee-keepers, until very recently. In the primitive condition of our forests, and in earlier times, the very nature and instincts of the honey bee, prevented injury from this source. The woods had not yet been cut down, nor become familiar to the tread of man. Swarms of bees from different settlements, and of distinct blood, became near neighbors, as they emigrated to the woods and found homes in the hollow trees. Thus strengthened physically by constant foreign mixture, and stimulated by the great blossoms in unfelled forest trees, the westward march of the honey bee, in his colonization of the forests, was far more rapid than that of the squatter or the emigrant. Although man, the Indian, and the bear, attracted by the accumulated stores, proved alike—the enemy of the hive, the honey bee continued to thrive and increase, until under changed conditions, a deterioration naturally succeeded from destruction of natural pasturage, and injury from in-and-in breeding.

"As civilization advanced, and men owned small sections of woodland every part of it became well-known to the owner or to the ubiquitous hunter. In such communities every 'bee-tree' was soon marked and destroyed. Thus all prospects of new blood, naturally from emigrating swarms, was destroyed, as colonizing swarms in the woods decreased, either from lack of suitable trees in well settled communities, or from speedy destruction by those who sought their stores.

"Superstitious notions on the part of old fashioned bee-keepers tended greatly to augument the difficulty. If a man wished to make a start in bees he must either *steal* a hive from the *nearest* neighbor, or get it from the woods near by, for it was generally thought the bees be moved but a small distance. The result was that the bees in any one vicinity continued to increase *without new blood*. In many places the distant to the nearest bee-keeper was too great for mixture in mating, or else the neighbors around stole a hive from the man who first started in bees. Thus breeding from the same stock from generation to generation, it was no wonder that a general complaint was heard: 'Father's, or grand father's bees used to do well here; but some how, in late years, they have run out.' Every observing bee-keeper has met with similar experience in his own observations amongst 'old box hive' bee-keepers. The importance of this subject in bee-keeping, seems fortunately to have been stumbled on while working for other ends.

"Simultaneous with the introduction of movable combs, and such increase of practical knowledge as tended to advance bee-culture, the claim of the great superiority of the Italian bee, led to its being imported, bred, and largely desseminated. Without now entering upon the subject of the comparative merits of the Italian and native bee, it is enough for the present purpose, to state that we believe a great deal of the acknowledged good from the introduction of Italian bees into apiaries, all over the country, comes from the *introduction of new blood.* We are satisfied that the Italian bees are, in several respects, superior to our native bees, but not according to the apparent improvement when our Italian queen is introduced into, and bred from, in our apiary. Many men whose bees had deteriorated from in-and-in breeding, have found such superiority when an Italian was introduced as to run to the opposite extreme, of overrating these new bees. The controversy among the different apiarians at present, concerning the comparative merits of the two varieties hinges, as we believe, just on this point. Those who claim superiority or equality for the common bee, are parties who have, to some extent, reared Italians, or else some of their neighbors have had them, and thus the stock of common bees they have had on hand, have been improved by the new blood, which they do not feel is due to the Italians, because their bees are black bees, or merely hybrids, from black queens, and Italian drones. It is well known that some prominent breeders have claimed that the hybrids are, in many respects, superior to Italians. We believe that the ordinary apiarian will find it more profitable to get an Italian queen, and from her raise *only* queens; permitting them to mate with black drones, than to get both *the drone and the egg for the queen from the same queen*.

QUEEN REARING.

Pure Italian queen rearing is important to apiculture in our country, more for the benefit of new blood, than because of the superiority in the bees themselves. But those who rear them, in order to get the best bees, must not continue to breed from the same queen, and her direct progeny, because of bright color; but must constantly introduce new pure Italian blood, into their breeding departments, both from abroad and from other apiaries in our own country. But, for the interest in the Italian bee, perhaps not for a long time to come, would bee-keepers have learned to cage, ship, import, and introduce queens as they have, thus opening up a way for improvement in the bees themselves, as well as in modes of management for profit. The conclusion which we have reached on this subject is this: Encourage the Italian queen rearers, so that they can, and will furnish good, pure stock, and at the same time introduce new blood—the best blood you can get for hard work in the apiary. It may be that still greater results may be gotten from introducing, and crossing the Dalmatian, Cyprian, and Egyptian bees, with those we now have. Seek improvement in bees, just as in stock, by mixing and crossing and continuous breeding in pure strains for crossing with others.

CHANGING A STOCK OF COMMON BEES TO ITALIANS.

To Italianize a colony of black bees, it is only necessary to remove the native queen and substitute in her place a fertile Italian queen. The Italian queen will commence laying almost immediately, her progeny beginning to hatch in about three weeks, and in from three to six months the whole stock will be pure Italian. The native queen is most easily found by opening the hive near the middle of a clear day, when many bees are absent in the fields. Handle the combs carefully, looking over one at a time, using the smoke sparingly, lest the queen be driven from the combs. It may sometimes be necessary to shake the bees upon a sheet, that the queen may be seen and destroyed as she crawls toward the hive. If the Italian queen was obtained from a distance, the box in which she was shipped should be opened before a window, in a closed room, that the queen be not lost should she fly from the box. When introducing a choice queen, we should run no risk of having her stung by the bees; she must therefore be confined in a small wire-cloth cage, which should be immediately inserted near the centre of one of the brood combs, where the bees will cluster upon it, feeding the queen and keeping her warm. A drop of honey placed within her reach can do no harm. At the end of thirty-six hours, she should be liberated, smeared with honey, and allowed to crawl down among the bees.

Another method is to remove the native queen, and if near the swarming season, look for queen cells and destroy them if any are found. The stock is now allowed to stand queenless for about ten days. Open the hive on the tenth day, at the farthest, and cut off *all* the queen cells, for if longer neglected a queen might hatch which would have to be hunted up and destroyed. The bees being now without eggs or young larvæ, will give up all hopes of rearing a queen, and the Italian may be safely introduced as before directed. In all cases the queen should be well smeared with honey before she is allowed to go among the bees, as while cleaning off the honey they have no disposition to sting, and having time to discover her *rank*, receive her kindly.

In the proper seasons a populous stock may be divided and an Italian queen caged and given to the queenless part, or a swarm may be driven from a strong stock in the box hive, as directed on page 60, and after returning the native queen to the parent stock, the Italian queen may be introduced to the swarm in the new hive. Again, a queen may be given to a natural swarm after hunting out the black queen. If another Italian queen cannot be had, the black queen should be returned to the parent stock.

ITALIANIZING A WHOLE APIARY.

"*A man near Gotha, Germany, purchased two stands of Italian bees five years ago, and in the spring of 1866 had increased his number to twenty-five stands, not one queen of which had mated with the black drones, though hundreds of common colonies were within two miles of him. His secret is to keep his colonies always very strong, not aiming at a rapid increase, and making his swarms very early. The instinct of the Italians is to rear drones earlier than the other bee, and they rear brood much faster in the spring, so that it is safe to 'do' the swarming before the black drones appear, and thus secure the impregnation of your young queens by Italian drones.*"—PRAIRIE FARMER.

If the colonies are in box hives, transfer one or more strong stocks and obtain queens for them any time during the season from May to November. In order to commence with pure stock, the queens should be obtained from some reliable person, as almost every subterfuge is resorted to by unprincipled dealers to make the public believe that *they*, above all others, have the location for breeding pure Italians. Early the next spring, place drone comb near the centre of your Italian stocks, and feed them regularly to induce early breeding, and bring the drones forward several weeks before black drones appear. If your black bees are in common hives transfer them, putting the drone comb in the outside frames. Should you desire to Italianize stocks for neighbors, they may be brought to your yard and Italianized with your own. As soon as the Italian drones begin to hatch, form one or more strong nuclei from your best Italian stock to obtain a large number of queen-cells, as directed on pages 65, 66 and 67.

On the eighth day after forming the nuclei, examine to ascertain the number of queen-cells, and remove the black queens from about two-thirds as many stocks. Leave them thus over night to realize their loss, and then carefully insert a queen-cell among the brood in each stock. Mark the frames containing them and examine the next day, for if any are destroyed others must be inserted in their places. What queen-cells remain may be used for other stocks, except to leave one in each nuclei to hatch and become fertile to supply neighbors or to be used in swarming. This method is short, but requires close attention to prevent some stocks from rearing black queens or becoming queenless. The stocks will also be somewhat weakened by being deprived of a laying queen even for a short time at this season of the year. The process will seldom be so well managed but that a few black drones will be reared, hence if queens are not reared early the first season, some of them will be likely to mate with black drones, which will be known by some of their worker progeny having but two yellow bands and others none at all, while a part will have the three bands of the pure Italian. A few poorly marked in any stock should not condemn it, if there are any hybrid stocks in the yard, as bees from different colonies will mix to some extent; but the young bees should be examined when just hatching from the combs, to see if all have the three yellow bands. If any queens are found to have mated with black drones, it is safest to remove them as soon as other queens can be reared to take their places, for although they will produce pure Italian drones, yet should such a stock swarm or lose its queen, a queen would be reared (unless prevented) from her hybridized eggs whose drone progeny would be impure.

Another method preferred by some, is to Italianize all your own and your neighbors' stocks as far as practicable the first year. To do this, secure the construction of as many queen-cells as possible from the brood in the Italian stock, and insert one in each nucleus. Let the queens hatch and become fertile, paying no attention to what kind of drones they meet. When fertile introduce them to the parent stocks, and rear others the same way before swarming. These queens, having been fertilized by black drones, their *worker* progeny will be hybrids, but their drones will be pure. The next season, all the drones in the apiary being pure Italians, the work is half accomplished. Then rear another set of queens, one for each hive, from the original pure one, and there being none other but pure drones in the neighborhood, the young queens will seldom find black ones, especially if the apiary be large.

ITALIAN QUEEN REARING.

The superiority of Italian bees is becoming so generally known that there is a great and constantly increasing demand for queens; hence the necessity for plain practical directions that shall insure success in rearing them even by the inexperienced bee-keeper. We are aware that general rules have been given, and many nice things written, yet the practical part, upon which success depends, is understood by but few. We have already given directions for rearing queens to Italianize an apiary, but when desirous of engaging in their extensive propagation, the following course should be pursued. Having Italianized your own apiary, and all your neighbors' stocks within about three miles, you are fully prepared to commence the business of queen rearing.

SMALL BOXES FOR THE NUCLEI.

The small hives or nuclei boxes should be made about six inches square inside, and the same in depth below the rabbets, which should be three-fourths of an inch deep. The frames, four in number, are suspended upon these rabbets, their top bars being narrow, the same as the side and bottom bars. The movable cover should be an inch larger than the top of the box, and clamped to prevent warping. Listing, or strips of woolen cloth, should be tacked all around on the under side of the cover, near the edge, to fit upon the top of the box and confine the heat generated by the bees. Before nailing the box together, a rabbet, five-eighths deep and two inches wide, should be cut across the inside of the back, and a piece tacked on the lower edge to hold in the tin feed trough. One end of this rabbet must be filled up and the other end covered with a flap screwed to the outside of the hive.

This flap is to be turned to admit of drawing out and filling

---

NOTE.—We now use only large hives for queen rearing, having discarded the small boxes.

the pan when necessary to feed, and when the bees are to be confined to the hive, turn the other end of the flap, which should have a hole in it covered with wire-cloth, to give ventilation. The boxes should be painted a variety of bright colors—some white, others red, blue, &c.—and scattered over the yard so that a young queen may easily distinguish her hive from any other near it. A cheap stand is made by nailing strips of board for posts to each corner of a bottom-board eighteen or twenty inches square. The posts should project eight inches below the bottom board, for legs, and two of them sixteen and two eighteen inches above it, laying on a board for shade. We make the small frames the proper size to fit four of them into one of the large frames, and thus obtain brood from any hive by filling the small frames with thin worker-comb, or sticking in small pieces and allowing the bees to build the combs. We prefer, however, to have one or more *breeding hives* made the same as the small hives, but long enough to hold sixteen of the small frames, and having several entrances along the front side.

HOW TO COMMENCE QUEEN REARING.

As soon as drones can be reared in the spring, break up the stock from which you wish to breed, and transfer the combs into the small frames, placing them on the old stand in one of the long breeding hives. Shake the bees upon a sheet near the entrance, and as fast as they enter and collect on the combs they may be lifted out and placed in the nuclei boxes, giving a frame of brood and one of honey to each, and filling the other two frames with empty comb.

Each nucleus should have about one quart of bees, which must be closed in, laying a rough board on the top and turning the flap to give ventilation. To prevent them from returning to their old stand, they must remain closed in for about thirty-six hours, when the entrance should be opened at sunset, the ventilator turned, and the regular cover put on to retain the heat. If bees for the nuclei are taken from a natural swarm, or brought from the distance of a mile, they need only be confined until sunset. About three quarts of bees must be left with the old queen in the breeding hive, and it may be necessary to place upon it the cap of the old hive that the bees may recognize their old location and not enter other hives. If queen-cells are at hand, one should be inserted when forming each nucleus; but if none can be had, leave all the nuclei until the tenth day, when more nuclei may be formed and a queen-cell for each taken from those first formed, leaving but one in each nucleus. Examine the nuclei often after queen-cells are inserted, as some cells may be destroyed or prove worthless and others be needed in their places. As soon as any nucleus hatches its queen, one of its empty combs should be exchanged for a frame of brood in the maggot state from the breeding hive. This will stimulate the queen to make her excursion to meet the drones and *prevent the bees from following her*, in which case, unless discovered, they would be lost. The brood, if supplied often, will also keep up the strength of the nuclei. It will be found convenient to have a piece of slate or board attached to each nucleus upon which to record its condition. When a queen becomes fertile, it will be known by eggs being found in the brood combs.

SHIPPING QUEENS.

The simplest way to send queens is by mail, in a small wooden queen-cage, containing sugar candy poured when hot in one end for food. It is best to enclose twenty or twenty-five workers with her. Such queen cages are made by boring one and one-half inch auger holes nearly through a plank one and one-fourth inches thick and cutting into blocks two inches square. A small auger hole for an entrance on one edge, stopped with cork, and a wire cloth tacked over the hole completes it. We have sent queens by mail successfully to the Sandwich Islands. Sometimes it may be preferred to send queens with comb and brood in nucleus boxes by express. If so, one small frame of bees and honey is sufficient. Fasten it securely, so as to prevent possible injury, and give good ventilation, (with opening, covered with wire cloth).

REMARKS.

Except where queen rearing is followed as a business, we recommend using only full sized frames for nucleus hives. They are then exchangable at any time, and may be used for full colonies in winter.

When small frames are used the *outside* of each should be a certain proportion of the inside of the full frame, so as to be used within it when desired for placing in the full hive.

Whenever there is a scarcity of honey in the flowers, it will be necessary to feed some of the nuclei, especially those having unfertile queens or young brood, and those constructing queen-cells. Also the breeding hives, as it is sometimes necessary to keep the bees continually building comb in order to induce the queen to rear much brood.

A regular supply of queen-cells may be had every five days by having two queenless stocks, and inserting in them alternately every fifth day, comb containing eggs and larvæ taken from any stock from which you may wish to breed. The queen-cells must be removed by the tenth day from the time the brood was inserted, lest a queen should hatch and destroy all the other cells in the hive. If the comb containing eggs and larvæ for queen-cells be new, more cells will be built. Before inserting it in the queenless stock it should be cut in strips an inch wide by three inches long. To insert one of these strips, make an opening in the comb three inches long by one inch deep, and directly under this cut out a piece two-and-a-half inches long by one inch deep, which will give room for lengthening down the cells, and also leave a shoulder to support each end of the strip. As fast as the cells are used other strips may be inserted in the same openings. A queen is seldom injured while caged if the wire-cloth be neither coarser nor finer than fifteen or twenty meshes to the inch. The cage is sometimes made by winding a piece of wire-cloth around the thumb and stopping the ends with corks, but we prefer them made about three-eighths of an inch deep, nailing the edges of the wire-cloth to a wooden bottom. When introducing a queen, the cage is sometimes suspended in the hive by a wire between two combs, but the safety of the queen is better secured by inserting the cage in a comb near the brood, with room above for the bees to hover upon it.

By making and keeping stocks queenless, and feeding them when necessary, drones are retained for fertilizing queens late in the fall. By inducing the bees in such stocks to cluster outside, either by contracting the space inside, or leaning a piece of comb filled with capped brood against the entrance, drones will collect to such hives by thousands.

CHAPTER VI.

THE APIARY.

In selecting a site for an apiary, we prefer to have the ground descend slightly to the east or south. The hives should be protected in winter and spring from the prevailing winds, either by buildings, trees, fences or other breakwind. Although we prefer, when convenient, to have our hives front the east or south, it is of little consequence as far as the prosperity of the bees is concerned. The hives should be sheltered from the rays of the noonday sun, except in April and May, when much warmth is needed to promote breeding. Care should be taken not to place hives *against* old buildings or fences, which form a congenial harbor for bugs, spiders, ants and other insects. Each stock should have a separate stand, and there is no danger of getting the hives too far apart. It is most convenient to have the hives near the ground. From five to ten inches is high enough for stands if means are taken to keep down the grass and weeds. A cheap and good stand is made by taking two pieces of four inch scantling fifteen inches long, and nailing upon them a board twenty inches long by fifteen wide. If a higher stand be preferred, take, instead of the scantling, two pieces of joist two inches by six, or four pieces of board may be nailed

THE APIARY. 125

together with a fifth one across the top, forming an inverted box. These stands oeing movable, the stocks are less liable to be crowded, and when most convenient may be placed in an orchard, as there should be low topped trees and shrubs near the hives, both for shade and for swarms to cluster upon. The hives should also be in full view from the most frequented part of the house, that swarms may be heard and seen as they rise, with the least possible trouble.

LARGE APIARIES.

In choosing a location for a large apiary, the pasturage afforded by the neighborhood should receive attention—such as white clover, orcharding, forest trees, &c. If this be satisfactory it will pay well to go to some expense in fitting up a bee yard. One hundred stocks conveniently arranged, will need little more attention than ten managed in the ordinary way. If the situation be a windy one, a yard should be enclosed for the purpose. Let the fence, especially on the north and west sides, be about seven feet high, and tight if practicable. This will not only be a great protection in winter, but will break off the cold raw winds of spring, and thus save the lives of thousands of industrious workers that would otherwise be blown to the ground and perish at the very threshhold of their homes. Stands should next be attended to. These should be a few feet away from the fence to give room for passing behind the hives. An excellent arrangement for stands is to set two rows of short posts, of some durable kind of wood, letting them project but four or five inches above the ground. Upon these, lay scantling or small timber, forming two parallel lines about fourteen inches apart. Cut bottom-boards twenty inches long by fifteen wide, and lay them across and on the top of the scantling, observing the proper spaces between the hives. Next, procure sawdust or spent tan, and fill up under the scantling and around the posts. This will effectually keep down the grass and weeds, keep the hives clean, and prevent the frost from heaving up the posts. A shed should also be erected over the hives, both for shade and shelter from storms. In whatever style this is put up, it should be but five or six feet high, and open all around, so as in no way to interfere with working around the hives. The roof need be but four or five feet wide, and should slope toward the front of the hives. If there be no water convenient, a supply should be furnished the bees during warm, dry weather. It should be pumped or poured into a shallow trough containing small stones or shavings, for the bees to alight on, and changed often.

BEE-HOUSES.

Of bee-houses we deem it hardly necessary to speak. They are regarded as unprofitable by our best apiarians. Some of the objections are, cost of construction, danger of crowding hives too close, and consequent loss of young queens when returning from their nuptial excursions, and lack of a free circulation of air in summer. Beside, they afford numerous crevices and lurking places for moths, spiders, roaches, and other "unclean birds."

HOW TO PROCURE BEES TO STOCK AN APIARY.

First, by Purchasing Bees.

Old stocks in box hives may be purchased and transferred into movable-comb hives. We prefer those not over three or four years old, that have cast swarms (and with them their old queens) the year before, unless the black queens are soon to be destroyed, and the stocks Italianized.

Smoke and examine them. If in the spring, they will, of course, be less populous than in the fall, yet bees should be clustered between most of the combs. The combs should be free from mold, and are easier transferred if in broad sheets. The less drone comb the better, and the more honey there is, the more you will have left for the table after transferring. We have transferred stocks from large box hives, giving them an abundance of honey, beside leaving out enough to amount in value to the purchase price of the stock. But if stocks that are not to be transferred, have, in the spring, from twelve to twenty pounds of honey, they will usually swarm earlier and be more prosperous than heavier ones, as large quantities of honey, at this season, only take up room that should be occupied with young brood. Probably the best stocks to purchase, are second swarms of the year before, provided the hives are full or nearly full of comb. Such stocks have young queens, and the comb cells are the small size proper for rearing workers, as drone comb is seldom built during the first year of the queen's existence. But if your hives are left to be filled with new swarms, take first swarms by all means, being careful to get, if possible, those from hives that have swarmed the year before, as such will have vigorous queens but one year old. We could not advise the purchase of second swarms at the time of their issue, unless early and of fair size, for except in good seasons, many fail to secure sufficient stores for winter.

In purchasing bees care must be taken in removing them home. It should be only early in the morning or late in the evening if warm, else many active workers will be lost. A new swarm having tender comb filled with honey should not be moved, for such comb will be apt to break down.

By Taking Bees on Shares.

Bees are sometimes taken on shares for a term of years, the person taking them finding hives and getting half the increase and honey, or more, when transferred into movable-comb hives and Italianized.

By Capturing Fugitive Swarms.

We once bought twenty stocks, at five dollars each, of a man who got his start by finding a swarm hanging to a bush. Fugitive swarms may often be brought down by throwing dirt among the advance guards, or by getting in the proper position and reflecting the rays of the sun upon them from a looking-glass.

By a Safe Increase of Stocks.

After a few stocks have been obtained, by any of the foregoing methods, by far the cheapest way to stock an apiary, is to increase the number of stocks by nucleus swarming, and obtaining bees *gratis* of neighbors, by taking up their condemned stocks in the fall. Such swarms are taken home and supplied with frames of honey.

By using Surplus Honey Stored in Frames.

Our best apiarians all agree upon one thing, which is, that bees will store more honey in the body of the hive than they will in top boxes. For this reason, and the advantages in supplying needy stocks for winter, we prefer to have a part of the surplus stored in frames. Whenever honey is taken from the hive, it should be set into boxes or hives, and taken to a dark room and kept until fall, when some may be needed in preparing stocks for winter. Some should also be kept on hand for emergencies, and the rest may be sold or used in making new colonies with bees obtained

By Taking up Light Stocks for Neighbors.

There are enough in almost any community who are so far behind the age as to hive their late swarms in box hives without uniting them. These and other light stocks they brimstone in the fall, *unless* they can get the "bee man" to take them up for the bees. Every bee-keeper whose apiary is not fully stocked, and all who wish to make the most money out of their surplus honey, should prepare to take as many such swarms as they can supply with frames of honey to winter upon. The process of taking up a swarm is nearly the same as for transferring. Have a small box with a hole in each side covered with wire-cloth for ventilation. As each comb is taken out brush the bees to the entrance of the box, and when all are in close it up. As it does not pay to winter small swarms, we usually put two or more together, and if no queens were removed all but one will be killed. The empty combs are valuable to use in honey boxes and frames in the body of the hive, and may be purchased at the market price of beeswax. Fasten them into frames with melted rosin, and use them to fill out the hives after giving each swarm four or five combs of honey. If this be not done the space should be contracted by inserting a partition board or a frame with a cloth tacked upon it. Each swarm should also have some bee-bread, which may be got by exchanging with old stocks.

HUNTING WILD BEES.

We have known many persons to get a start by lining wild bees to their trees, which, if cut in spring or summer, the bees will do well. Transfer them with their combs into movable frames, the same as from a common hive. We have cut trees where the bees entered seventy or eighty feet from the ground, with no small timber to break their momentum in falling, and yet saved the swarms. After a tree has been cut and the swarm hived, bees from neighboring swarms will soon appear, to take charge of the waste honey, and if more wild swarms are in the vicinity, which is usually the case, they are easily followed home. By taking lines from the different trees as they are cut, several may often be found within the circuit of a half mile. Bees are found with the least trouble in February or March, when they fly out on the first warm days, and some becoming chilled fall upon the snow. Lines taken from buckwheat and other flowers should be carefully marked, and if not traced up at the time, may be found towards spring by the dead bees on the snow. When a tree is found, cut upon the bark, (in the least conspicuous place,) your initials, with date of finding, and let it stand until drones appear in May, when, if the queen should be killed in falling the tree, there will be eggs in the combs from which to rear another, and drones for her fertilization. When the bees are at work upon the flowers a line may be started by taking a plate or a piece of board, upon which is a small piece of comb filled with diluted honey. You will also need a glass tumbler and a piece of brown paper or dark colored cloth. Having found a bee upon a flower, place over it the tumbler and leave it inverted upon the cloth till the bee rises to the top. Wait till it quits buzzing, (that it may not get besmeared with the honey,) then carefully raise the tumbler and place it over the honey on the plate, wrapping the cloth around the upper part of the tumbler to darken it. The bee will descend toward the light, when, coming in contact with the honey it will commence loading up. Gently remove the tumbler while the bee is at work, and stepping back a few feet, place your eye near the ground. With the clear sky for a background it is easy to keep sight of the bee as it rises, describing several circles at first, then striking a "bee-line," for home. It soon returns with many others. When a strong line has got to work, cover the bees with the tumbler, and moving them along the line towards the tree again liberate them. Care must be taken not to go beyond the tree, else the bees may not return. If the tree is now supposed to be near, mark the line of bees by setting an assistant stick, in range, a few stakes. Again cover the bees upon the plate and carry them a few rods *away from the line* in order to get a *cross line*. Mark this also with stakes, then run out both lines by sticking more stakes, and the tree will be found where the lines meet. To find the place where the bees enter the tree, walk slowly backward and forward in its shadow so as to bring every point of its body and large branches in range between the eye and the sun. Look at the sides of the tree and outwardly, just below the sun, where the bees are easily seen and appear quite large from the reflection of the sun's rays upon their wings. A spy-glass is a great aid when the bees enter high up in the tree. In the fall or early spring, when the trees are bare of leaves, it is easiest following lines and finding the place of entrance in the tree. With a little honey or dissolved sugar for a *bait*—which, if not poured into comb, must contain some floating substance to keep the bees from drowning—lines are readily started from "sugar camps," or moist places, outlets of springs, &c., where the bees come for water. In the gathering season it is sometimes difficult to get bees to work upon the bait unless new honey be used, taken directly from the hive. The honey, if not very thin, must be diluted with water, else the bees may not leave directly for home. To attract the bees, choose the middle of a warm sunny day, and going into the edge of a field or other open place as near the supposed locality of the wild swarm as possible, burn a piece of dry comb or beeswax upon which a little oil of anise has been dropped. In half an hour or so the bees will come following along the line of smoke, where the bait should be placed, scented also with anise oil to aid the bees in finding it. The bees from the richest tree are not the most hungry, but fly cautiously and angrily about before alighting. If the bees are got properly to work, one or more swarms may often be found, which, if transferred into hives will be a valuable acquisition, but are too often thoughtlessly destroyed for their stores alone.

HOW TO TRAP WILD BEES OR ROBBERS.

We give this method more especially for pioneers in a new country, for although a *part* of a swarm or swarms of fugitive or wild bees may be easily trapped without finding the tree, by getting them to work upon a bait, yet if other bees are at work within reach *there is no way to prevent catching them also, even though they belong to your own or your neighbors' apiary.* After getting into the supposed vicinity of wild bees, and a mile or more from any apiary, get the bees at work upon a bait by either of the methods given. Remove the cap and frames from the American Hive and place in it the bait containing plenty of honey, with the bees upon it. Close the entrance, leaving open the two fly-holes above it. Set another hive upon the top of this one, having first bored a hole in its bottom for the bees to pass up through. This hole may be covered with a slide to be worked through a hole in the side of the hive. The hive should also have wire-cloth tacked over its top and the cap left off, as in moving bees. After a strong line of bees have got at work, going and returning, close one of the fly-holes of the lower hive and insert in the other a tin tube about six inches long. The outer end of the tube should not project beyond the front board, and should fit the hole to exclude the light. The inner end reaching to the centre of the hive should have a valve of light wood or paper hung to its upper side to cover the end. Open the door to the observation glass, and when enough bees have crowded into the hive to cover the glass, close the door and allow them to pass into the upper hive, which should be prepared to receive a swarm with frames in place, honey for food, and comb with eggs, from which to rear a queen, unless a fertile queen can be given it, caged, as in nucleus swarming. The piece of comb with eggs may be brought in a small box, with bees to keep them warm until needed. As often as the bees become thick upon the observation glass, close the door and draw the slide from the hole above, when the bees seeing the light will ascend into the upper hive. Should the bees cease coming before a good swarm is taken, open the other fly-hole near the tube and let some out till a strong line is again formed, being careful to have the slide cover the hole in the bottom of the upper hive whenever light is admitted into the lower one. A moderate sized swarm may often be taken without using the upper hive. After removing the hive to the apiary, let it stand closed till half an hour before sunset on the third day, when the queen must be uncaged and the bees allowed to fly. If no queen were given them, the hive should be opened in about three weeks, and the drone comb removed from the centre, if there be time to collect stores for winter, otherwise it should be left till spring.

MOVING BEES.

When moving stocks short distances, or only to different stands in the the same apiary, it should be done during a cold spell in winter or early spring, before the bees have fully taken their location.

If they are to be moved a mile or more, it may be done, with proper precautions, at any time of the year. The stocks to be moved should be prepared early in the morning or when the bees are not flying. To prepare a stock in a common hive, blow in a little smoke and carefully lifting the hive invert it upon the ground. Have ready four small strips of soft wood and a square piece of wire-cloth, or coarse cotton or linen, large enough to cover the mouth of the hive. Spread the cloth over the mouth of the hive, lay on the strips, and tack through the strips into the edges of the hive. These strips will save tacks and prevent the bees crowding out under the cloth. A sleigh, buggy, or spring wagon, is the best for moving bees, yet, with careful driving, they may be moved on a wagon without springs. Place the hives in the wagon upon a bed of straw, keeping them mouth up to secure ventilation, as bees need much air whenever disturbed. Beside, in this position the combs rest upon their attached portions and are less liable to break by jolting. If the weather be very warm use the wire-cloth to confine the bees, and keep the hives shaded from the sun. In most movable-comb hives, strips must be tacked across the frames to keep them from swinging together. To prepare a stock in the American Hive, simply remove the cap and tack the cloth or wire

136 TRANSFERRING.

cloth over the top. Drive upon a walk. New swarms may be brought home in a box in the cool of the evening after their issue, but if hives are left for them, and they are allowed to start *new* combs, great care must be used, if moved before the combs are finished.

TRANSFERRING BEES AND COMBS FROM THE BOX HIVE.

The best time to transfer bees into the movable-comb hive, is from the appearance of the fruit-tree flowers until swarming. During this season, when the bees are gathering honey, the beginner may safely undertake the operation, as the bees will promptly repair the combs and often be more prosperous than before. They may be transferred earlier, if carefully done, or indeed at any time, if the brood is not chilled by exposure to the cool air. Yet nothing is gained by disturbing bees in cold weather, neither is it safe to transfer for three weeks after a stock has swarmed, in which time its queen will generally have become fertile. But when a second or third swarm can be hived, and set close to the old stock, it is then quite free from bees, and may be transferred with but little trouble, and the swarm jarred from its hive and united with the transferred stock, making a

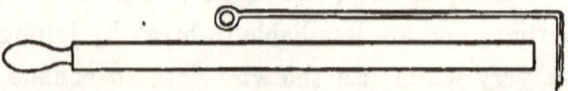

13. **Transferring tools.** The hook is to loosen the combs from the top of the hive or gum, when the side is not pried off. The other is made of a piece of hoop-iron, (2 inches wide by 20 inches long) by grinding the end bevelling like a chisel, and is used to loosen the combs from the sides of the hive.

good job. Or when an Italian queen is to be introduced, six or seven days after a stock has cast a first swarm, the old stock may be transferred and all the queen-cells destroyed, when the stock is ready for the Italian queen. The tools needed, beside those shown in the cut, (fig. 13,) are a hammer and stout chisel for prying off one side of the hive, and a long-bladed knife for cutting out the combs.

OPERATION.

Prepare the frames in the new hive, by prying off most of the comb-guides, and letting down the cross-bars to suit the size or the combs. After smoking the stock to be transferred, invert it in the shade, and, keeping the bees down with your "smudge," cut out a small piece of comb, containing brood, to place in an empty box or hive upon the old stand. Also, if other stocks are close, partially cover them to keep out returning bees. Our common practice (if in warm weather) is to drum the bees from the stock to be transferred, proceeding the same as in driving out a swarm, (page 57,) until the bees have ascended into the drum box, when it is removed and a cloth tacked over it, and left mouth up in the cool shade until needed. We now remove the old hive into a sheltered place, or, if flowers are scarce and other swarms near by, into a shop, out-house, or upon a clean barn-floor. Now drive out the cross-sticks, and with the hoop-iron sever the attachments of comb from the side of the hive upon which the combs run nearest parallel and can be most easily removed. Pry off the side of the hive with the chisel, cutting the nails if necessary, and commence cutting out the combs. Have a box, half the width of the hive, in which fasten some drone brood, and place it upon the *opposite side* of the hive from

---

NOTE.—We have found it most convenient to use fine wire for fastening in the combs.

which the combs are to be removed. The bees will gather into this as the work progresses. Lay a board upon a barrel, for a table, and upon this your transferring board, (18 inches long by 14 wide,) upon which two or three thicknesses of woolen cloth should be tacked. As each comb is cut out, brush off the straggling bees, lest they get besmeared, and lay it upon this cushion, and upon it your frame. Mark inside the frame, and trim off the comb in such a manner, that when fitted into the frame, it shall remain in about the same position (top edge up) that it occupied in the old hive, as many of the cells incline upward. Cut the comb a trifle large, and spring the frame over it. Fit in all pieces of good *worker comb*, even if old and black. Combs too thick to let the frames together, should be shaved off. The *drone comb* may be known by its large coarse cells, and unless placed in the upper part of the outside frames, should be rejected, by which a stock will often be rendered very prosperous that was no profit to its owner before. When transferred in the spring, no more honey need be put into the new hive than is necessary to secure all the worker comb, but if transferred late, plenty of honey should be given. As melted rosin or bits of tin are insufficient for fastening *heavy combs* into the frames, we use strips of wood, one-fourth of an inch thick by three-eighths wide. One of these slats is pushed under the comb, another laid on top, and the ends looped together with twine. Raise the end of the cushion-board, to bring the comb to an upright position, and set it into the new hive, which should be kept covered to exclude stranger bees. Care must be taken to place all combs containing brood or eggs, together in the centre, with the store combs next to the outside. If a comb be too weak to sustain its weight, it must be divided in the middle, and the upper half supported by a cross-piece tacked within the frame.

If the air be cool, the bees in the small box set upon the hive, will be needed to keep the brood warm in the new hive, and may be shaken into it when only two or three frames have been filled, but in warm weather, we usually transfer all the combs before hiving the bees. If there be much honey in the combs, it is well to place a shallow pan—made for the purpose—beneath the frames, to catch the drippings. If this be not done, clean off the bottom-board with a wet cloth. Cover the upward passages to keep the bees below, and bringing the drum box, shake the bees on a sheet at the entrance of the hive, (being careful not to jar the combs,) gently brushing them until all have entered. Keep the hive in a vertical position, and carry it steadily (without the cap) to the original stand. Blow a little smoke under the box left to hold the returning bees, and, if numerous, jar them upon a sheet in front of the hive. Replace the cap, contract the entrance, and shade the hive from the sun.

When the bees are gathering but little honey, and there is no out-building into which the stock may be taken after drumming out the bees, place a board upon a sheet, and upon it your drum box, and cut out all the combs before transferring them into the frames. As the combs are removed, one by one, brush off the bees upon the sheet, and let them enter the drum box, while an assistant immediately carries the comb into the house, placing it upon a few thicknesses of rags. As soon as the bees have entered the drum box, set it upon the original stand, and let it remain until the combs are transferred into the new hive. Then hive the bees as directed. In this way, there is little danger of robbers, or losing the queen, and the brood is not liable to be chilled in the warm room. Late in the season, when the bees are rich in stores, and consequently harder to control, the beginner may sprinkle a few grains of tobacco upon his rags for smoke, being careful to subdue the bees at the start. If the flowers are not yielding a supply, feed the scraps of honey to the stock the next morning, placing them in the chamber of the hive, as much honey is consumed in elaborating wax to repair the combs. In four or five days after the transfer, the temporary slats are to be removed, and any crooked comb straightened. For convenience, we fasten a permanent loop to one end of a slat, and a piece of wire to the other end. The other slat is left smooth, with one end slightly sharpened, to push under the comb when the looped slat is laid on, and the loop slipped over the sharpened end of the under one. Give a twist to the wire at the other end, and the comb is secured. The slats are removed by drawing the smooth one out of the loop, which loosens the other, and both are drawn out. These slats may be used many times over, and will last for years.

ROBBING.

Early in the spring when few flowers have appeared, and after they fail in the fall, or indeed in any time of scarcity, weak and queenless swarms are apt to be troubled by robbers. Yet the prudent bee-keeper, by caring for such stocks in time, will avoid the danger. When flowers are scarce, expose no sweets near the apiary while the bees are flying, as "prevention is better than cure." Robbers may be known by their buzzing around the hive in a very suspicious manner. Should one alight, he is hurled from the entrance and frequently receives the fatal sting As long as this state of things continues and the attacked colony is prompt in defending itself there is little danger, but should the robbers gather about the entrance in considerable numbers, they may be dispersed, for the time, by sprinkling with *cold water;* but if the attacked colony be very weak, or not discovered until resistance has ceased, it should be closed (ventilating well) and either taken from home until the danger is past, or carried to the cellar or a cool room, and fed diluted sweet for three or four days. When again placed upon the stand, the entrance should be carefully guarded. If a half inch block be placed upon each side of the entrance and a piece of lath or shingle laid across, robbers will be cautious about entering the shallow passage. A short board leaned against the front of the hive, is also an excellent protection. Should it happen that a powerful stock from a neighboring forest attacks a colony, remove it as before, and trap the robbers as directed for capturing wild bees. A handful of long grass laid over the entrance, will assist a weak stock. The robbers get entangled in it and are more easily driven away. A piece of glass leaned against the hive over the entrance will often check their depredations. In either case it is best to contract the entrance so as to admit but a single bee at a time, and elevate the rear of the hive, so as to give the attacked bees the advantage of an inclined bottom board.

THE MOTH-MILLER.

We regard the fear entertained of the moth-miller as misdirected and more imaginary than real. As long as a stock is strong and in good condition it is safe, but should it be suffered to decline from over-swarming, loss of queen, or other cause, the eggs of the miller are allowed to hatch in the exposed combs, and as the bees die off from natural causes the moth-worms increase, and (if not dislodged) finally gain entire possession. The female miller is much larger than the male, and resembles in color a sliver from a weather beaten fence rail. During the day, she may often be found sticking about the cover of the hive. Toward evening, she will be flitting about the entrance, and if the combs are not covered with bees, or cracks and crevices can be found, or litter is retained on the bottom-board, she will be at no loss for a place to deposit her eggs within the hive. There can be no "moth-proof" hive; but if the entrance be on one side only, and the bottom-board is inclined, the bees have all the protection against these intruders that a hive can afford. *Moth-proof* hives (so called) are owned either by persons of little information, or sold to such by unprincipled venders, as well informed bee-keepers know how to prevent the ravages of the moth, and also know that in warm weather, more or less moth eggs are present in all the combs. Hence, a real moth-proof hive must also exclude the bees. During the summer months, if a mixture of vinegar and water, well sweetened, be placed at night among the hives, in white dishes, many millers will be drowned. Moth "traps" form the basis of a considerable trade. Some of these might be well enough if they were empted and the worms destroyed every week; but as they are usually neglected, they become "moth nurseries," instead of traps.

Worms may be trapped early in the season, by laying pieces of shingle or split elder, the hollowing side down, upon the bottom-board. The worms will retreat under these to spin their cocoons, and must be destroyed once or twice a week, or they "take unto themselves wings and fly away." The moth is less troublesome in large apiaries. The sprightly little wren, if encouraged to build its nest near the hives, will destroy myriads of worms and insects. They are easily attracted, by putting up boxes made three inches square, with an inch and a half hole for an entrance.

ANTS AND OTHER VERMIN.

Ants will frequently get into the chamber of the hive if not properly constructed, and whenever disturbed are very annoying to both the bees and the keeper. *To banish them from the hive* start them out with smoke and brush a little *spirits of turpentine* where they "most do congregate," and should they have a hillock near treat it a few times to *warm soapsuds*, and the ants will bid you a long adieu. If spirits of turpentine be not at hand, the leaves of catnip, tansy or black walnut, placed in their "retreats," will usually drive them away. Spiders often spin their webs about the hives and ensnare some bees. They should behunted out and destroyed. The large mother wasps appear singly early in the spring to start their nests, and each, if not prevented, is destined to be the parent of a *little swarm*. They often harass the bees, and should have no quarter. At the approach of winter, the mice may seek a nesting place in the warm hive. If there are holes large enough to admit them, they should be contracted or covered with wire-cloth.

TO PRESERVE HONEY COMBS FROM THE MOTH-WORM.

As long as honey combs remain under the protecting care of the bees, they are secure, but if removed from the hive in the heat of summer, the eggs of the moth already upon them will hatch, unless prevented, and finally destroy them. How the eggs get there, is a question. One theory is, that they are deposited by the miller upon the bottom-board and about the entrance, and occasionally adhering to the feet or legs of the bees, are thus carried among the combs. The other is, that the miller is allowed at times to visit every part of the hive. One thing is certain. If in summer, we drive out all the bees and close the hive to exclude the miller, hundreds of worms will be developed, in from one to three weeks, acording to the temperature. The same is sometimes true of honey in the surplus boxes, though in a lesser degree. When removed early in the season, if to be kept in the boxes, it should be noticed frequently, and if small lines of a fine white powder are seen upon any of the combs, expose them to the fumes of brimstone. To do this, prepare a match by dipping the end of a cotton rag into melted brimstone, and when no arrangement for smoking has been made in the honey room, take a store box or flour barrel, and leaving a cavity at the lower end to receive the match, put in the boxes in such a manner that the smoke can enter them, and cover the top to confine the smoke. When separated from the combs by straining, honey is secure from the moth, its food being wax, and not honey. Strained honey may be kept from graining, by heating to the boiling point, (setting the vessel in boiling water, to prevent burning,) and keeping it in a dark room. Empty combs, unless the moth eggs have been destroyed by freezing, should be examined occasionally, and if traces of worms can be seen, smoke them also, being careful afterwards that millers do not get to them.

WINTERING BEES.

In regions where the ice garb of winter remains unbroken from fall till spring, the consumption of food may be lessened, and the safety of light stocks better secured by wintering them in dry cellars, or even in houses. But in this changeable climate, where the bees are frequently aroused to activity by summer weather in the middle of winter, and impelled to fly out to discharge their feces, it is not so necessary to guard against cold, as it is against the great consumption of honey in warm weather, or the filth and disease caused by confining the bees where they can be affected by changes of temperature in the atmosphere. Hence, unless a *dark*, *dry* cellar can be had, the mass of bee-keepers at least, will succeed best by properly preparing their stocks, and leaving them upon their summer stands.

WINTERING IN THE OPEN AIR.

In October, the exact condition of all the stocks should be ascertained, both as to their strength, and their supply of stores for winter. If any are found lacking in both these points, join two together, or strengthen them with bees obtained from neighbors, (page 88,) and supply them with extra food. To ensure the safety of the stocks, till flowers bloom in spring, each should have twenty-five pounds of honey. With a little practice, the amount of stores may be very nearly determined by inspection, or simply by removing the cap and lifting the hive from the stand. However, if the combs are more than one year old, there is much liability of being deceived, when judging by lifting or weighing the hive. The reasons are, that old combs are heavier than new, and often contain large quantities of bee-bread. Still, the experienced bee-keeper will seldom err in his estimate of winter supplies. Should any lack stores, give them reserved frames of sealed honey, or if this cannot be done, and other stocks are very heavy, exchange a frame with each. If the lower part of such combs are empty, they may be placed near the centre of the needy stocks, as there should be honey directly above the bees; but if full, place them a little to one side of the cluster, for the reason that bees need empty cells to winter in. The comb in each frame should have an inch hole cut through it, four or five inches from the top, to enable the bees, in extreme cold weather, to reach the stores in the outside combs without danger of freezing, by leaving the cluster to crawl around the edge of the frame.

Over the summer quilt place a woolen quilt or piece of carpet or other woolen material, and above this place an old bag filled with chaff (or other absorbing material) to absorb the moisture arising from the hive. It is neceesary to secure upward ventilation through the holes near the top of the upper box without a draft.

This will absorb the moisture generated by the bees, thus keeping the combs dry and free from frost, while it permits the foul air to pass off so gradually that cold currents within the hive are avoided. Stocks standing in exposed situations, may be greatly benefited by enclosing the hives (except the entrances) with caps made of flags or rye straw, being careful to exclude the mice. Set up a broad board to shade the hive, and especially the entrance, during the middle part of the day. If this be done, the bees will seldom leave the hive when the air is cool enough to chill them. When a judicious method of swarming has been pursued, and the colonies properly cared for, they should be populous and well provisioned for winter, requiring little trouble in preparing, or risk in keeping them safely through till spring. Such stocks, if shielded from the piercing wintry winds, and properly ventilated, will pass a Siberian winter uninjured. Bees should not be disturbed during winter, except at the close of every long spell of cold weather; when, if the air be warm enough for them to fly without being chilled, open all the entrances to their full capacity, allowing the rays of the sun to strike the alighting board, when the bees will fly out, void their feces and return, without loss, to the hive.

This is the greatest difficulty in northern bee-keeping. In the far South bees often gather pollen and honey, at times through the winter months. In such climates there is but little danger of loss in winter, unless their stores are almost exhausted when the cold season comes. But in the North, and especially in the far North, the bees gather nothing from the fields for fully six months. Many experiments in wintering have been made, within the past twenty years. At that time, and even later,, the principal writers recommended wintering in cellars, but more recently the tendency everywhere, except in the far north, where continued uninterrupted cold weather lasts a long time, has been towards wintering on the summer stands.

Throughout the Middle and Southern States we recommend only this kind of wintering. If hives are properly prepared with gentle upward ventilation, absorbing material, a supply of young bees, sufficient good stores, and protected from the cold winds and unseasonable sunny days, there need be little fear in wintering.

PREPARATION FOR WINTER.

This should be begun before the last honey season is over. See that every colony has a good young fertile queen. Unite weak and queenless stocks. See that each hive has from twenty to thirty pounds of good honey, with combs, which also contain bee-bread, for rearing young bees. If later stores have been gathered from honey-dew; cider mills, refuse from sugar refineries, or if the fall honey is very acid, they should be extracted, and the hives supplied with combs of good dark honey, set aside in summer with the honey from unsealed boxes, or they should be fed with sugar syrup. Give in such cases from five to ten pounds of sugar to each colony.

Make a syrup, putting one part of water, by measure, to two parts of sugar; let it come to a boil, to be sure that all has desolved, and feed it in suitable feeders in the cap. Give it to them warm. Any kind of a good feeder, with floats to prevent drowning, will answer.

A good way is to fill quart fruit jars with the syrup, tie over the mouth a piece of cheese cloth, or other strong thin material, and invert directly on the top bars of the broodnest; packing the quilts around well, to keep in the heat. Sometimes two or three jars will be drained in a single night. If there is sufficient brood in the hive, feed rapidly, so as not to induce too rapid breeding. But if there is little or no brood present, the feeding should be more slowly, to induce breeding, for a *plenty of young bees* is one of the important elements in successful wintering. In sections where there is little or no fall honey to stimulate the queen, we would advise extracting the honey, from at least a few of the central frames, and stimulate so as to go into winter quarters with a fine supply of young bees, as well as a plentiful supply of good stores. There is no better winter food than syrup made from nice A sugar. At this season out door feeding must not be practiced, because the stronger colonies, which least need it, will get the most, and often so fill up the brood nest, that there is not a good nest of empty combs in which to begin the winter.

This feeding, when practiced, should be completed before cold weather sets in, in earnest. October is the time to complete it. If the hives are to be wintered indoors, the cellar or winter house should be dark, dry, of equable temperature, not lower than forty, nor greater than sixty degrees. A number of colonies in the same room, will help to keep up the warmth of the cellar. A small ventilation shaft, opening without, with a damper to regulate the draft, will give ventilation in the room. If in a cellar, under a dwelling, a small pipe from the cellar, connected with the pipe of a stove in use, will keep the air dry and pure. The hives should be moved into the cellar with great care, to prevent jarring, so soon as cold weather sets in, in earnest, and remain until it is well over, even to May, in very cold latitudes, though they should be set out, a few at a time, for a fly on some warm day in midwinter. They should not be taken permanently from such indoor winting places, before the very bleak wintry winds are over. If a mistake is made, and they are set out, before severe weather is over, it is, we believe, best to return them to their quarters, if it should suddenly blow up severely cold, as much loss is apt to ensue.

When wintered in cellars, much upward ventilation should be allowed. The cap may be left off, and a piece of fine wire-cloth tacked on, so as to prevent the depredations of mice. On this, quilts, or boards may be laid, covering partially, according to the strength of the colony. Strong colonies require more, and weak ones less ventilation.

Evidently this mode of wintering requires a great deal of labor and *timely* attention. Sometimes with the best care the bees will become restless, we know not why, and will always need a fly during winter; many people have no such suitable cellar, and they are expensive if made, or they may not well answer the purpose, owing to the nature of the soil. For these reasons, and the ease of wintering on summer stands, almost everywhere in our country, except, perhaps, in the extreme northern sections, we recommend generally to winter on summer stands. In rather northern climates we recommend air chambers around the bees, to prevent sudden changes in the weather. After hives are prepared with stores, and otherwise for winter, we recommend that they be packed for winter in this way: Reduce the frames to six or eight, according to size, for bees winter better when the chamber is not too large for the size of the colony. Remember this fact, in preparing for winter, that bees can stand *cold*, but that they cannot stand *dampness* Arrange so that the moisture, generated by the bees, can gently escape upwards, through some absorbing material, without giving a cold draft of air. This condition is attained in several ways of packing, when holes are made in each end of the upper chamber, to allow ventilation. It is attained by placing chaff cushions at the sides and over the brood nest; by putting over the hive an extra box, packing between the two with absorbing material, or by placing above the quilt two or three thickness of cotton batting, or a bag of chaff, saw dust, or something of the kind. We would recommend that the absorbing material used be always in a bag, to prevent littering up the hive, unless pads of cotton batting are used. Perhaps, nothing is better than this. The honey board above confines the moisture so much to the hive as to endanger it in cold climates. A good cushion for both sides and top of a hive, is made as follows: Take a bag, a little wider than the depth of the hive, from front to rear, fill it with chaff or cut straw, so as to be two inches thick all over. Tack a few stitches here and there, as in a mattress, to hold the chaff in place. This may be of proper length simply to fit tightly in the upper box, or longer, so as to reach the bottom on each side of the frames over division boards. The latter is preferable in rather cold climates, or where wide hives are used. Contract the entrance and turn up the alighting board, to keep the sunshine from the entrance, so that it may not tempt them from the hive, when it is too cool for them to fly freely. The entrance should never be over a quarter of an inch deep, so as to check mice. This can be supplemented with auger holes above, which for winter can be stopped with corks.

Thus arranging for winter is less trouble than moving into cellars, and the hives are always in place. Turn down the board from the front a few warm days, or open from the caps, if snow is deep, and the bees get a good fly naturally, without mixing up, as they often do when set out for a fly. The labor of moving out, and returning several hives to the cellar, is considerable, and the warm day may be most inopportune,—just when some other business is pressing, and the bees must be neglected. There is less danger from "spring dwindling," and on the whole we would recommend out door wintering. It is well always to have the hive on the south-east side of a good evergreen hedge, or high, tight board fence to break the force of the cold penetrating winds. If convenient, extra coverings for winter are useful; but they should be such as are easily removed as spring opens, so as to permit the rays of the sun to shine directly on the hive in April and May, to promote breeding.

There should, by no means, be permitted any cracks in the cover or sides of hives through which rain or wet may beat or drive. Dryness is an essential condition, else combs will mould, and conduce towards dysentery, whether in the cellar or on the summer stand.

In preparing for winter, half inch holes should be cut put in the centre of each comb, two or three inches below the top bar, and one or two strips laid across top of the frames, under the quilt, to procure free passage of the bees from one comb to another, in very cold weather. In the North this is very essential, but not so important in the South. Whether chaff cushions, straw, thick quilts of batting or other absorbing material be used, the quilt should be put over the bees first and the packing afterwards. A plain piece of ducking is perhaps as good cloth as any other for this use, as bees will gnaw it less than any other, except enameled cloth, which is both more expensive, and difficult to fold down close and tight to the sides of the hive. In Spring the absorbing material should be replaced by some warmer material, to better confine the heat.

FEEDING BEES.

Feeding bees differs materially from feeding other live stock. It is not absolutely necessary to feed at all, unless when stores fail in winter or early spring. Then no liquid food should be used. If no frames of sealed honey are on hand to give a needy colony, candy is the next best food for this season of the year. Sticks of plain white or clear sugar candy, thurst down between the combs, among the bees, before their honey is quite exhausted, will greatly lengthen out their stores. A half pound may be given at a time. It is cheap food, as a pound will last from four to six weeks. If a colony alive the previous day is found when most of the bees are apparently dead, they can usually be revived by sprinkling them with warm diluted sweets, and letting the hive stand a few hours in a warm room. They should then be given frames of honey or else fed. Box honey placed directly on the frames and covered well with woolen material will be appropriated in the coldest weather and save the colony.

It is always best to see that each hive has in the fall, sufficient stores for wintering, varying from twenty to thirty-five pounds of honey, according to climate or mode of wintering. Rather more honey is consumed on the summer stands, than if wintered in the cellar. It is well to set away some full combs of the dark and least salable honey in the summer to give to weak stocks in the fall. But if this has been omitted, they should be fed sufficient stores for winter, before it gets too cold. A syrup made of two parts by measure of A sugar, and one of water; fed warm in the cap each evening will be carried down very rapidly. Feed as fast as possible, to prevent too much breeding, and to prevent robbing. Feed regularly until the necessary amount is given. *Stop the holes in the caps whilst feeding*, especially if honey is used. Contract the entrance, and be careful not to drop honey or syrup about the hive, as much loss is sustained when bees rob and kill each other. This caution is necessary whenever feeding is necessary. In spring all colonies should be contracted by close fitting division boards; the combs being removed, except so many as the bees cover well Every few days insert an empty comb or sheet of comb-foundation in the centre of the brood-nest. Hives are thus built up very rapidly. If weak, or stores are insufficeint, they should be stimulated by *regular* feeding in addition. If there is present a plenty of sealed honey, they are stimulated in using it, if you shave off the caps a little at a time, from one of the outside combs. If stores are scarce, they should be stimulated by feeding thin sugar syrup, in small auger hole feeders, placed under the quilt, and filled by raising the flap from the hole in the quilt. They are thus stimulated to regular brood-rearing, when they would not enter feeders placed above the quilt for two or three days, in a cold spell. Good sugar syrup is much better than honey at this season of the year, because it does not so much induce robbing, whereby many bees are killed which can be illy spared at this important season. But we advise caution in the use of cheap grape sugar, because it often contains so much sulphuric acid as to ruin the bees. When bees fly before natural pollen is gathered, they should be fed with flour, as a substitute.

If no water is near, bees should, in summer, be watered regularly every day. A shallow trough with pebbles answers well. A good way is to invert large glass jars in plates. Only a small amount of water escapes around the mouth, and this is renewed as the bees suck it up. The glass is convenient to see the depth of water.

During honey droughts in summer, but little brood is reared, unless the queen is stimulated to activity by *regular* feeding. But if systematic feeding is pursued, especially with weak swarms, the hives are filled with young strong bees when the next harvest opens, and are enabled to secure much more surplus honey than if neglected.

FEEDERS.

In warm weather, almost any kind of a feeder, placed in the cap, with floats, to prevent drowning, will suffice. Good floats are made of thin boards, one-half inch less in size than the vessel. Nail a piece across the centre to prevent splitting, and with a coarse saw, slit the board in narrow strips, from each end to the cross piece. Three things are specially desirable in a feeder: That they be accessible for bees, without leaving an unnecessary hole into the broodnest, which permits heat to escape; that they be filled and examined, without the escape of a bee; and, that they be tight to prevent leaking.

Tin vessels of various kinds, have been made. These hold the honey well, but at times bees will not readily enter the cold metal, when feeding is desirable. Boxes of various kinds have been made, with entrances from below, and close glass tops. These answer a good purpose. Frames or boxes with duck cloth bags, are sometimes used, but they are in the way in the broodnest, and if used above, the syrup often crystalizes in the cloth and makes it stiff. The simplest feeders are made with the auger. Take a strip of two-inch board, six inches wide and with a one and a half inch centre bit bore two auger holes three-fourths of an inch apart, from one edge nearly through to the other. Near the back end, bore with the same auger, directly in the division between the two nearly through. This connects the two and makes a hole for pouring in the food from the top. Tack in it a wire cup, made by bending over the thumb a piece of wire cloth, to keep back the bees when feeding. On this division near to the front, bore with the same auger holes one-half inch deep, side by side, nearly to the front, and in the centre of the division, bore three-eight inch auger holes through to the bottom for entrances. Tack four strips on the bottom, to give entrance to these, and a strip over the auger holes in the edge, and it is done. It may be set directly over the hole in the quilt, and a piece of glass laid over the entrances. Other holes may be made side by side, and the feeder as large as desired. The entrances need be only between every other hole. If preferred the entrances can be made on each edge of the block, at the upper edge of the auger holes. In this case the strip to cover the auger holes must be narrowed to suit. Such entrances are best for feeders made with three-fourths inch augers, in inch boards to place directly on the frames, under the quilt, for early spring feeding. As many holes as desired may be made side by side, and connected by the division being bored away from above. A piece of glass laid over these holes, will give a view of the interior. Simple, cheap, and excellent feeders, can thus be easily made, which will answer all the purposes of the apiary.

We have lately seen a very valuable feeder, made by J. M Shuck, of Des Moines, Iowa. It consists of a block of wood two inches square and thick, and as long as the frame, three deep grooves run from end to end. The end pieces close the ends of these grooves and extend one half an inch above. A top bar is put on and it sits in the hive like a frame. It is filled by a wire cloth thimble from the top and this closed with a piece of tin, which turns on a nail.

PROFITS OF BEE-KEEPING.

Bees are kept for profit, pleasure, or recreation; and as a means of promoting or regaining health. Unlike other live stock, they are self-supporting. They not only provide their own food, but with little care, will store a large surplus of their delicious product.

How much easier it is to give bees the little attention needed, than the trouble and expense of caring for cattle, pigs, and sheep, three times a day, which no good farmer complains of. It is indeed strange, that any person, occupying a rood of "mother earth," should neglect so rich a source of profitable enjoyment. Could our young men and young ladies, who now spend hours in idleness or vain amusements, be induced to purchase a swarm or two of bees, and give them the little attention needed, it would not only prove highly remunerative, but would lead them into habits of industry and thoughtfulness, and fit them for better citizens. By the introduction of improved hives, a fresh interest has been awakened in this branch of rural economy, and with honey at present prices, there would undoubtedly be a general rush into bee-keeping, were it not for the fear of stings, and a vague belief that "luck" has something to do with successful bee management. A little practical knowledge with regard to the nature of bees, will enable any one to obtain perfect control over them, and will also open his eyes to the fact, that, with properly constructed movable-comb hives, success in bee-keeping is not left to "luck" or "chance," but depends upon the observance of simple rules and regulations. With such hives, the bee-keeper is enabled to ascertain the exact condition of a stock at any time, and thus remedy defects, or easily remove any comb in the hive for any purpose whatever.

A few stocks of bees are often entirely neglected, and consequently less profitable, while a larger collection (needing little more care) receive proper attention; when the profits, as from farm products, will mainly depend upon the season.

"The intelligent, practical bee-keeper, can take care of five hundred swarms, and make a portion of the hives needed for new colonies."—*U. S. Patent Office Report.*

"The profits resulting from a judicious and proper system of bee culture, may be safely estimated at from one hundred to five hundred per cent. per annum. I have three swarms, which have paid me in honey and increase of stock, upwards of $100 in two years. The average profit upon my entire stock, for three years, has been three hundred and twenty-seven per cent. per annum, or $3.27 has been the annual profit on every dollar invested." —*Dr. Eddy.*

"On the 25th of April, 1858, I purchased ten hives of bees, in the old fashioned box hive, for $50. They were so full that I had to divide them before I could move them. I divided the ten, and made me twenty hives. On the thirteenth day after, I divided ten again. I took four queens from one hive, in the cells, and ten from another, and gave each swarm a queen-cell, which hatched the next day, making thirty hives. I sold from those thirty hives, $547 worth of honey, and the increase of my bees is worth $500 more, making $1,047 in one year, from an outlay of $50. I took from one hive, twelve frames filled with honey, in fourteen days, and I had a number of hives from which I took twelve frames, filled with honey, in twenty-one days."— *E. Townly, Cincinnati, O.*

The "American Agriculturist" gives the results of the apiary of Bidwell Brothers, of Minnesota, for two years past. In

1864, their apiary consisted of one Italian, and fifty-eight stocks of black bees. The one Italian stock was increased to fifteen. and the fifty-eight stocks of black bees to one hundred and eighty-one, principally by artificial swarming, and averaged 42½ pounds box honey per stock; while, for the past season, from two hundred and four old stocks they received, on an average, a trifle over seventy-five pounds surplus honey per stock.

"A. Kearns, of Grundy County, started in this business, with a single swarm in an "old gum" owned by a neighbor, of whom he received half the proceeds for keeping them. One hive, one year old, filled three boxes that weighed as follows: one 34½, one 35¼, and one 36½ pounds, boxes and honey together, and the fourth partly full. This bee business is of growing importance. As soon as these discoveries are thoroughly known, bee raising will become as general as any other branch of production. When men learn that it is just about as cheap to raise honey as not to raise it, and far cheaper than to buy it, they will no longer avoid the business."—*Prairie Farmer*.

Let a person estimate the profits of bee-keeping, by commencing with a few stocks, and on an average, doubling every year, or putting the yearly average of surplus honey per stock very low, compute the interest accruing from capital invested in bees, and consider how easy it is to accumulate such capital, with the fact that constant attention is never required, and that hives will last almost a lifetime, he will not be surprised to find the most intelligent men in this country and Europe, turning their attention to apiarian pursuits.

CHAPTER VII.

DIARY OF HONEY PLANTS.

Success in bee-culture depends upon various things, just as success in every other line of business. The farmer who aims to keep a few hives, in some neglected corner, and who "has not time" to attend to them at the proper season, cannot expect to find the bees very profitable. He can no more expect a large income from *them*, than he could from his corn which he "had not time" to work, after he had planted it.

But whilst this is true, careful and timely attention is, perhaps, nowhere better paid than when judiciously given to bees. This chapter will be devoted especially to the different ways in which that which is pleasant an ornamental around the home, may be made also profitable for honey.

FRUIT TREES.

Every home should be surrounded with fruit trees, unless so restricted by walls and streets in the city, that there is no room for them. Every farmer, from year to year, should increase the number of fruit trees. The value of fruit for health can hardly be over estimated. Bees are very important in securing a good yield of fruit. Sent by nature, from flower to flower, they carry the pollen and fructify the germ, and make a good crop more certain.

A few years ago bees were banished from a certain town in Connecticut. under the impression that they injured the fruit; but, in less than two years, the edict was removed, because their loss was felt in the failure of the fruit to set, and all were convinced of the wrong done the bees and the bee-keeper.

Cherries, peaches, pears, and apples, furnish the first good honey harvest. Every bee-keeper should therefore have his orchards to build up the bees first, and afterwards repay well in fruit for many years and sometimes for generations. Fruit trees are almost the only kind of farm produce which continue to bear for the next generation.

Fruit trees of all kinds may be obtained of nurserymen, but we advise always to purchase direct, and not from peddlers, who will often deliver them at the most inopportune time. If one is not able to purchase, they may be raised from the seed and grafted the second year, or buds or grafts may be inserted on any natural stocks. Good dry soil is best for fruit trees. Let it be well worked as if for a crop, and then given a good dressing with manure. A few words may be useful concerning the mode of planting: The holes should be dug large enough to hold the roots without bending from their natural position. The finest and best soil should be worked in and around the roots; filling every space and bringing every root fully in contact with it, so that no opening is left among them. If very dry, a pail of water should be added, and dirt drawn up a little higher than the surrounding soil, and packed down firmly with the foot. It should not be planted deeper than it stood in the nursery after the ground settles. If in an exposed position the tree should be staked and tied firmly to it with a band of straw or other material. The first summer all fruit trees should be mulched with coarse manure or litter, from three to six inches deep and extending a foot or two farther in every direction than the roots. In a fruit orchard a hoed crop is greatly preferable to any other, for the first five years. After this start, fruit trees will grow and produce fairly in turf.

The cherry tree thrives best on a sandy or gravelly soil, but succeeds well in almost any situation except a wet one. It is one of the most ornamental of fruit trees, and claims a place in the yard and garden. It thrives well anywhere along the fence or hedge. Bees work rapidly on it in the Spring. The plum attains its greatest perfection on a strong, clay soil, where they grow most thriftily and suffer least from "curculo."

The peach is of easy culture, and of such rapid growth that where wood is scarce it may be grown advantageously for fire wood. Of this fruit it is not necessary to speak. A warm, sandy, and dry soil is the most desirable location for this fruit. The soil should be moderately rich, and if convenient, on rather high land, having a northern slope.

Orchards may be well arranged with peach trees alternating with standard apples or pears. The peach yields first and by the time that the apple trees need the ground they must be cut out.

Fruit trees of all kind may be planted either in the fall or spring. In cold climates, where they are in danger of freezing out, it is best to wait until spring, and then carefully set out as early as the ground will permit. The fine roots should not be permitted to get dry, but be kept wrapped in some soft, moist material. If once thoroughly dried in the sun, the growth is retarded, if the tree is not injured.

SMALL FRUITS.

First among these stand the Red Raspberry. It is a very profitable crop, when grown convenient to market. The raspberry succeeds best in a moderately rich, mellow soil. It should be planted in rows five or six feet apart, and well cultivated to produce the finest results. The roots of the raspberry run near the surface of the soil, hence care must be taken not to plant too deep. Soon after the fruit trees, it yields an abundance of beautiful honey, for two or three weeks. The honey is secreted rapidly and bees work on it throughout the day. In damp, rainy weather, bees visit its blossoms, when scarcely anything else seems to be yielding honey. Blackberries, currants, strawberries, and gooseberries, are visited by the bees, but among these for purposes of the apiarian, none compare with the raspberry.

BASSWOOD.

This tree is too well known to need any description. It yields rich, light honey, from July 10th for about two or three weeks. In large portions of America it is found in abundance, in the natural forests along with the poplar or tulip tree. Different varieties of the poplar bear the name of white-wood, which yields honey in abundance in May and June.

SOUTHERN HONEY TREES.

In the South the orange and lime trees, sour-wood, poplar, holly, and persimmon, yield large quantities of honey. In some parts of North Carolina and Virginia the persimmon is found in great abundance. A writer from Henderson county, N. C., wrote some time since to the MAGAZINE as follows, concerning it:

"The persimmon affords plenty of honey where it is abundant. Swine eagerly hunt for the urn shaped flowers when they fall, and thrive well on them. This tree does not injure the growth of grass or crops near it. The fruit is liked by many persons. Bees go a long distance

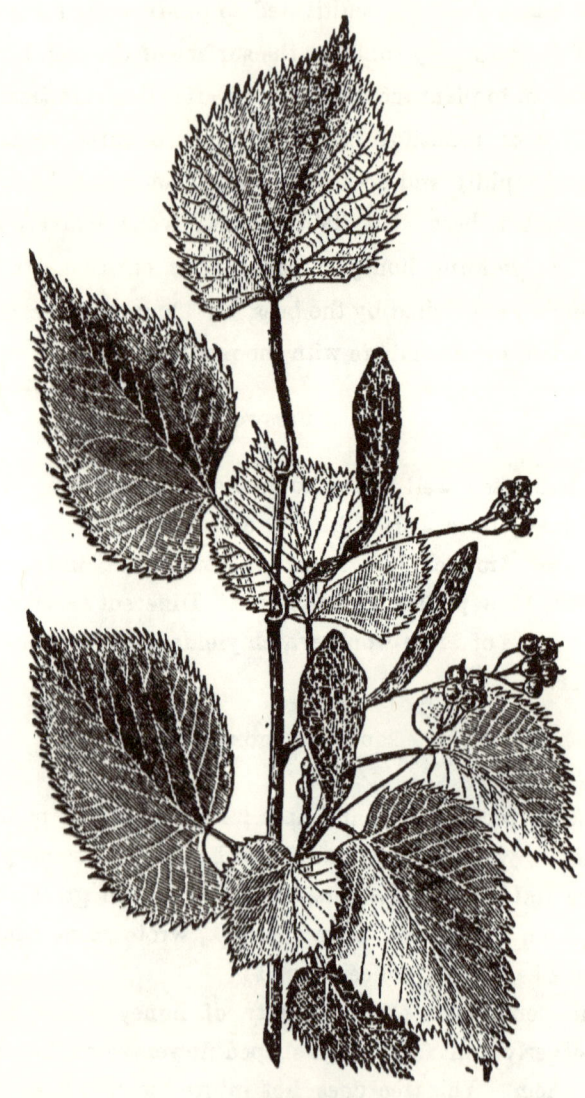

BASSWOOD.

to revel in its white fringe-like flowers, of a delicate odor, resembling honey scented with anise. It is one of our finest honey plants."

It blooms in spring, soon after the fruit trees cease to yield their honey. Rev. James W. Shearer, formerly of Virginia, tells us that through many of the poorest parts of Virginia and the Carolinas, the persimmon tree abounds, and describes it thus:

"It is a tree seldom found in the forests, but abounds in waste land throughout many parts of Virginia and North Carolina. It grows from twenty to forty feet in height, and is peculiar in this respect, that when left for shade, the soil around and under the tree is enriched, and grain will grow even up to the roots better than in the surrounding soil. The fruit, which is a very sure crop, is unfit for use until after heavy frost falls upon it on the tree. When fully matured in winter it tastes very similar to the date of commerce. In many section where the persimmon abounds the land can be bought at very cheap rates."

THE ORANGE.

In the far South, where the orange is grown, bees gather honey from its blossoms in abundance, whilst northern bee-keepers have their hives in the cellar or covered deep in the snow.

THE SOUR-WOOD, OR SORREL TREE.

The sour-wood is a small tree, abounding in the natural forests in many parts of the South, from Virginia to Georgia. It grows from twenty-five to forty feet high, and in the early summer is full of fringes of blossoms, which afford large amounts of the most beautiful and delicious honey in the world. Each little blossom somewhat resembles the cup of the lilly of the valley, but somewhat between it and the mountain laurel in appearance. The tree is covered with these little cups, which are so rich in honey that it is pleasant to suck the honey from the blossoms. Rev. J. W. Shearer tells us that he has often, whilst riding along the road, broken off bunches of the blossoms and sucked them, to get the refreshing honey, or shaken the honey from their cups into his hand and eaten it. He declares it to be in flavor and appearance superior to any honey with which he is acquainted. It is a slow growth, and the wood is hard and firm. The general growth of the tree is somewhat like the dog-wood.

In addition to the above mentioned shrubs, and trees there are many which produce much honey in different parts of our broad and diversified land. The first place must be given to basswood and sour-wood, among honey producing trees, and these followed by the magnolias, orange, lemon, locust, maple, the poplar or tulip tree, white-wood, red-wood, fruit trees of all kinds, the persimmon, the button-wood, the butter bush, chestnut, the Judas tree, black gum, mezquith, and many others.

SHRUBS—RASPBERRIES.

First among shrubs stands the raspberry, and of these the red raspberry is the best for honey. In the South the andromedas of different kinds, known by various names as "heathworths," "bee meadow," and "leather leaf," are more profitable for honey.

THE SUMAC

yields an abundance of good honey wherever it is found. There are in some sections two varieties—the early and the late. Both are shrubs growing from five to fifteen feet high. The early variety has red berries when ripe, and the late, yellow berries. The early sumac begins to bloom in June, and lasts from three to four weeks. The blossoms coming out in succession. The later variety blossoms in August and yields good pasturage for two or three weeks. This plant is found in great abundance in many parts of our country. It has become of considerable importance as an article of commerce. The leaves are gathered, dried and ground. It is used extensively for dyeing purposes.

The willows and alders are very timely for bees in spring. Besides these there are a number of shrubs of great local importance to the bee-keeper's success, the witch hazel, hawthorn, the wild crab apple, blackberry, wild cherry, the Virginia creeper, the bush honey suckle, St. John worts and many others. Each bee-keeper should study well the flora of his own locality and manage his bees with discretion according to the expected honey flow.

The only general advice we would give concerning the cultivation of trees for honey, beyond that given on page 155, is once more to call attention to the importance of good fruit on every farm, and the necessity for shade trees for stock. Where the persimmon abounds, its peculiar character of not impoverishing the soil, makes it a most excellent shade tree for cattle, at the same time a treasure to the bees when in bloom. The locust should be planted along lanes and in spare places, because of the great value of its timber for posts when cut, as well as for bees whilst growing.

PERENNIAL PLANTS.

First among these stand the clovers—white and alsike. White clover is two well known to need any description. It should be sown among other grasses for pasture land. If sown alone it takes from eight to twelve pounds to the acre. It begins to yield honey about the first of June and continues from four to six weeks.

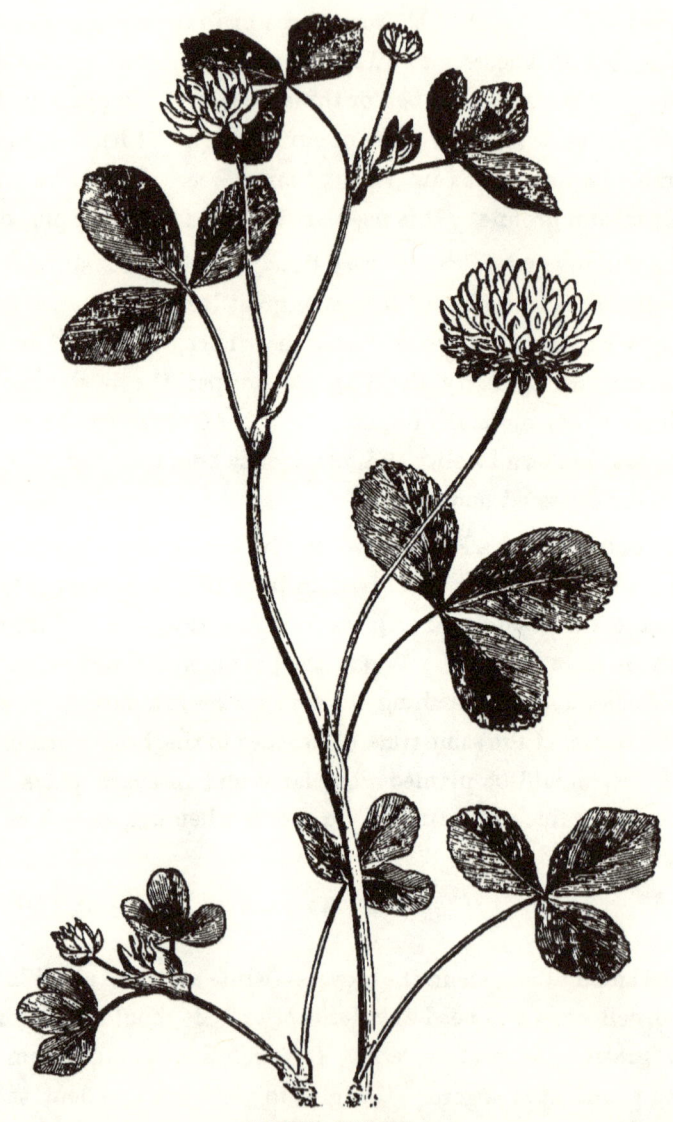

ALSIKE CLOVER.

Alsike clover seems to be intermediate between the white and red in size of growth and also in the size of color of the blossom. The seed is only about half the size of red clover seed, and it requires only half as much by measure to sow an acre. In other respects alsike clover is sown and treated like other clover. In sowing only from five to seven, pounds per acre is needed. It seems to furnish richer pasturage than red clover and at the same time has all the advantages of white clover for honey. When cut at different times during the summer, it yields an abundance of honey. The seed is still high, and as it is growing in favor with farmers the demand for the seed is so great that the price is good. It succeeds best in a cool, moist, loamy soil.

Lucerne seems in some sections to yield honey in abundance, whilst others report that they have it in abundance, yet have never seen bees at work upon it. Sow as clover, with from twelve to eighteen pounds per acre. It may be that some do not consider it a honey plant because during its season other honey, which the bees prefer, is so abundant that they neglect it, whilst in other sections they visit this plant in quantities. These remarks apply not only to lucerne, but to many other bee-plants, which in other communities are not visited by bees. This insect is very choice—like a boy at dinner. Let him commence on dessert and he will be content to make his whole meal of cake, pie, and puddings, to the neglect of potatoes, bread, and cabbage, So Bees will always work on that plant which they find at the time preferable for honey in the vicinity, to the neglect of other good honey plants, which would be visited in the absence of the first. Again, another reason why certain flowers yield much honey in one vicinity, and not in another, seems to depend upon the nature of the soil and climate, yet we are unable at present to give more than general reasons, which the progress of the bee-keeping industry must examine, and settle so far as possible. It is well known that certain flowers yield honey all day and others, only in the morning. Some secrete it only in moist, warm weather, and others, in cool weather.

Fruit trees fail sometimes to yield honey in cold, cloudy weather. Buckwheat yields none of consequence in very hot and dry, or in very wet weather. Many have noticed that in two fields, side by side, which have been managed differently, bees will be found thick on the blossoms in one, whilst not a bee is seen on the same kind of blossoms in the other. And besides, many have noticed that one season bees work greedily on a plant, which they will not touch another year. The reason may be either,

First. Because for some cause affected by climate or soil, there is no secretion of honey one year; or,

Second. Because some other blossoms at the time yields more honey which the bees prefer.

Extremes of cold or heat, wet or dry weather are apt to seriously affect the flow of honey, and besides flowers grown in hard poor soil oftimes yield much less honey than others of the same kind near by in soil which is in good cultivation, moist, and fertile. So many different things, climatic and otherwise affect the honey flow, that we should not too suddenly conclude that any given plant does not yield honey because in one particular locality, under one management, and in any particular year it failed to produce honey as we expected. This whole field is a comparatively new one, and one which may well claim careful study by apiarians in the future.

MELILOT.

Melilot is a handsome plant; but it is uselesss, except for ornament and for honey. It yields finely, but when established becomes a very troublesome weed. It is an annual. We mention it here because of its popular name—*sweet clover*. Sow three or four pounds to the acre.

MELILOT.

GOLDEN ROD AND ASTERS.

These fall flowers stand perhaps next to clovers among perennial plants as honey producers. Both the Golden Rod and the Aster abound in large parts of the United States. There are many varieties of each, yet neither are to be recommended for cultivation, because, like the Oxeyed Daisy and the Blue Thistle, they are looked on as weeds. They spring up in abundance in uncultivated fields. The Golden Rod may be known by its 'general appearance. It runs up in a stalk from one to

172 GOLDEN ROD AND ASTERS.

GOLDEN ROD.

three feet high,—a rod above the plant capped by a bunch of yellow flowers. It blooms in September, and in some sections furnishes an important part of winter stores for bees. In many places both the Golden Rod and the Asters abound, and as they blossom at the same time the honey is apt to be mixed. The Aster yields a lighter colored honey than the Golden Rod, when the weather is such as to secrete it rapidly. Few apiarians are aware of the immense quantities of honey which may be obtained from the Aster, because hives are generally filled with honey for winter, and the bees are not stimulated to active effort, and bees at this season are loth to build comb in boxes for storing it.

Since the introduction of comb-foundation great amounts of Aster honey may be gotten from the broodnest, by the use of the extractor. So soon as the harvest opens, remove all the sealed combs, and fill their places with sheets of comb-foundation. The bees are stimulated to the intensest activity. Every few days the honey should be extracted. When the harvest is over remove these new frames, to be kept for building up in Spring, and return the full combs for winter. It was from the white aster that Rev. J. W. Shearer secured, in Tennessee, such a yield in 1874. He commenced with one swarm, as reported in the MAGAZINE at the time, and in September and October extracted near five hundred pounds of aster honey, from five colonies, to which they had been increased during the summer, besides leaving a full winter supply in each of the five hives. With improved methods of securing this honey, it should receive more attention wherever this flower abounds. In the Fall the fields are white with the aster through many parts of the Eastern and Middle States. There are many varieties of aster called popularly by different names "Iron Weed," "Farewell Summer," "Rag-weed," "Stickweed," &c. in different regions. The Blue Aster is not so common, but is as good a honey plant.

BLUE ASTER.

The Aster grows from one to three feet high. It sends forth one main stalk, with several branches, each of which is covered with small white flowers, varying from one to five hundred blossoms on a stalk. They continue to open for weeks, until heavy frosts kill them. Slight frosts do not effect the blossoms, and bees can generally find honey in the late blossoms, until cold weather confines them to the hive.

BORAGE.

Of this plant, Mr. Langstroth says: "If there is any plant which would justify cultivation exclusively for bees, it is the borage. It blossoms continually from June until severe frost, and like the raspberry, is frequented by bees even in moist weather. The honey from it is of a superior quality, and an acre would support a large number of stocks."

CATNIP, MOTHERWORT, AND HOARHOUND.

These three plants blossom about the middle of June, and remain in blossom from four to six weeks. The flowers are very rich, and are visited by the bees at all hours and in nearly all kinds of weather. Mr. M. Quinby says: "In a few instances, I have known the catnip to last twelve weeks, yielding honey during the whole time. If there is any plant I would cultivate specially for honey it would be the catnip. I find nothing to surpass it."

Perhaps it is best to cultivate only such plants as are useful otherwise and incidentally yield much honey. Catnip seed scattered in fence corners, stony places, or along hedge rows, which are not kept in cultivation, will pay well.

TEASEL.

This plant is cultivated largely in some parts of New York for its dried blossoms, which are used by the manufacturers in taking the nap from cloth. It yields a beautiful honey in large quantities, but coming almost with basswood, cannot be cultivated solely for honey. It begins to bloom about July 10th, and lasts from twenty to twenty-five days—about a week longer than basswood. It is much thinner than basswood and beautifully white,—almost transparent when sealed up in the comb, but the flavor is strong and objectionable to many people.

BONESET OR THOROUGHWORT.

This plant yields honey during July and August, sometimes a little into September. In some localities and seasons it yields good honey very liberally.

Beside these, the whole families of mints, balms, and mallows are good honey plants. Plants of the genus *Cleome*, *Polanisia*, and *Sophauthus* abound in the great North-west, from Illinois to Oregon, and yield good supplies of honey. Early in the Spring bees are assisted in pollen gathering by the dandelion and crocus, which show their blossoms soon after the first warm weather sets in.

ANNUALS.

First in importance among annuals stands buckwheat, though not first in the quality of honey. Buckwheat honey is quite dark, but rich and good. This grain cannot be raised to advantage where the summer is long and hot. In cool mountanious regions the yield is best. Bees generally work on buckwheat during the month of August, unless the weather is extremely dry or wet. If an acre or two of buckwheat be sown a month or six weeks before the regular time for sowing it will yield honey for the bees just when pasturage fails in most places—from the middle of July to the middle of August. Sow from two to three pecks per acre, in May, June, and July, to yield the best pasturage for bees.

MIGNONETTE.

We believe that this well known fragrant favorite can be grown specially for honey with advantage. Its honey properties are well known, yet recent experiments have shown it more rich in honey than is generally believed. It is a hardy annual, and in good soil, in ordinary seasons, will bloom continuously until frost. About gardens, in borders, among shrubbery it is a favorite, because of its rapid growth, continued delicate blossoms, and fragrant smell. Bees visit this flower from "early dawn to dewy eve," and in all kinds of weather when they can fly. It should be sown in an open border, in April and May, and should be thined out or transplanted, giving each plant plenty of room. For cultivation, the plants should be in rows two feet apart—wide enough apart for the plow—and the plants some ten inches distant in the row. In good soil they spread rapidly, so as to cover the ground. If well thinned in this way, the plants will become much stronger and produce larger spikes of bloom. So far as we know all who have experimented with it, agree that properly cultivated for bee forage, it pays well. Mr. J. E. Johnson, editor of the *Utah Pomologist*, writes us as follows:

"After a continued experience of ten years I find that mignonette is the best honey plant I have found. It is almost as hardy, and blossoms as late as any honey plant, and is an ever bloomer, giving myriads of blossoms, and is covered continually by the bees. I find there is no plant that will furnish as much honey the year round, nor none that gives it better flavor. I believe that one acre of mignonette would furnish sufficient pasturage for one hundred stocks of bees. Certainly I have nothing in my list of plants, unless it is the English mustard, that bees work more freely on. Honey made from this plant has the most delicious flavor of any we have ever tasted, and where it has been tested in market, is far ahead of California or any other brands of honey and brings much higher price."

Mr. Wm. Thompson, of Michigan, confirms these statements generally, from his own experience in raising this plant, and adds, "Bee-keepers, after this, need not concern themselves about selecting a favorable location for their apiary. They can make it what they will, at very little expense. An acre of land put into good fertile condition, and planted in mignonette, will accomplish all that is necessary to render the situation as favorable as any that can be found. This adds another to the discoveries, which are rendering bee-keeping a thoroughly established science, and giving the bee-keeper an entire control of the situation."

The seed is about twice as large as that of the turnip, and it requires from one and one-half to two pounds to the acre. It can be obtained from any florist or from this office by the package, ounce, or pound. It costs about $1.50 per pound, twenty-five cents per ounce, or ten cents per paper. The established sweet varieties are, we believe, the best for honey.

MUSTARD AND TURNIPS.

Next to mignonette stands mustard, as one to be cultivated for honey. It blossoms at the time of the drought between white clover and buckwheat. It should be sown in Spring as early as the weather and soil will permit, planting from four to six quarts to the acre. It is best to sow it in drills one foot apart, though it is often sown in beds. In rich soil the stalks are from three to five feet high, and are covered with blossoms. This is not alone useful for honey. The tops make a good salad in early spring, and manufacturers of mustard for table use pay a good price for it. The black mustard yields honey most abundantly.

The turnip blossoms at the proper time to furnish good pasturage during the drought, just after the fruit trees yield is over. In the Southern States, when turnips are not winterkilled, the small ones left in the ground in the fall, will produce an abundance of flowers, rich in honey, at this season.

From the Northwest various annuals rich in honey, are reported such as Chickweed, Smartweed, Spanish Needle, Silk Poppy, the Minnesota bee plant, and the Rocky Mountain bee plant. Besides these a variety are found in almost every section, differing according to climate, which yield honey to a greater or less extent. Among these are the blossoms of melons, pumpkins, squash, and cucumbers, peas of different kinds, the snap dragon, the wild parsnip, which in some regions is very valuable, heaths, holly hocks, sunflowers, and many others.

Among all these there are none which we would recommend to be cultivated for honey save fruit trees, and raspberries, with basswood, and other superior trees from the list for shade trees, and groves; and as crops, buckwheat, mustard, turnips, and mignonette, as recommended before.

We must always remember that any given honey producing plant or tree does not uniformly secrete the same quantity of nectar one year with another, although it may be profuse in blossoms, since much depends upon the state or condition of the air and soil, during its period of bloom ; yet, it is also true that many plants blooming at the same time require very different conditions of the atmosphere in order to secrete the largest quantity of which they are capable, some require a dry, others a humid, and many an intermediate condition. This is a field for future examination and experiment.

CHAPTER VIII.

MONTHLY MANAGEMENT.

This department, the experienced bee-keeper will not so much need, as the beginner, for he has learned when to attend to his bees; but the novice continually needs *timely* advice and warning, least he neglect something, to the great detriment of his apiary. Even the experienced bee-keeper may be assisted in rendering prompt attention, by such a reminder; for all are aware how prone we are to neglect, or postpone, that which is of importance, unless reminded of our duty. We do not here propose to include everything which must be borne in mind, but will give general directions which will necessarily involve some repetition of what has gone before, which, we trust, is pardonable.

JANUARY.

Careful apiarians, by this time, have their hives all properly arranged, either in dry cellars; or, as we prefer and recommend, on the summer stands, as heretofore directed, unless in very severe climates. If wintered indoors, let the bees remain *as quiet as possible*; only examining occasionally to see that no mice are interrupting them. If on the summer stands, they should be examined often, guarding the entrance against mice, who love the warmth of the cluster, unless the entrance is so closed that they cannot enter. Throughout the winter a board should shade the entrance, so that the sunshine may not tempt them out, unless it is quite warm. If the alighting board be hinged to the bottom board, by two small staples, driven in opposite directions in each, it may be turned up when needed for shade, and turned down when they can fly. The board will prevent sun and rain from driving in at the entrance. Hives covered with light snow are protected in the best possible manner against cold weather, but when it begins to pack and freeze it should be removed from the entrance, or at least from the holes in the caps, when packed with absorbing material, as heretofore recommended.

Do no feeding in this month, unless the bees are about to run out of stores, and then give a frame of honey, or place honey boxes directly over the cluster. If these are wanting feed with plain white candy. If the candy is burnt in making it is not a suitable food for the bees. In warm climates these directions are not so important as where the weather is cooler.

During this and other winter months, the bee-keeper should prepare his hives, boxes and crates, and whatever is necessary about the apiary, so that he may not be pressed when the bees begin to need his attention, and perhaps the farm, orchard, garden, or other business calls for a share of his efforts.

FEBRUARY.

Keep the bees still as quiet as possible, where the weather remains cold and wintry. But if a warm day comes, uncover the entrance and let the bees have a good fly. They can then finish the winter, until the weather tempts them out. Any undue excitement by jaring or, in any wise disturbing them in cold weather, is very injurious. The bottom board should be cleared of all obstructions, and the dead bees swept out. If left, they injure the colony. If colonies wintered indoors show signs of uneasiness, they should be taken *quickly* to their summer stands on a warm day for a fly, and returned *quickly* in the afternoon, when they have ceased to fly.

In northern climates rye and oat meal may be fed, during February and March, in a sunny corner, protected from the cold winds: but in the South, natural pollen will be brought in during this month. After its appearance bees cannot be induced to use meal. Such feeding is useless, except in cold climates where the flowers are late in making their appearance. In the far South bees begin their spring work this month—gathering honey, and rearing brood, for the honey harvest and the swarming season is close at hand. Farther North, light stocks will need feeding, but where once commenced it should be continued regularly. When winter holds on well through February, no liquid food should be given, but candy or loaf sugar, as recommended for January. If bees are not permitted to fly during the winter, they are liable to dysentery. This disease is present whenever bees discharge their feces in a liquid state in the hive, on the bottom board, or on the combs. This disease seems to rise chiefly from feeding upon bad honey; increased, perhaps, by improper ventilation, or too great exposure to extremes of weather.

Bees have been retained in dry cellars for seven months, from November till May, without bad effects There is always danger from this disease when bees are confined to the hive for a long time without voiding their feces, and their food is inferior. Sometimes fall honey is inferior in quality, or bees being near apple mills, store in a great deal of unwholesome sweet, or else have a supply of inferior food gathered from the honey dew. The best way to prevent dysentery in winter is, to extract inferior or unripe fall honey and feed sugar syrup, as described in "September Management," or else substituting sealed summer honey in its place. But if at any time dysentery appears among bees in winter, they should be given an opportunity to fly and void their feces, as soon as possible. If the remaining stores seem to be bad they should then be fed with sugar candy, or if near spring, with sugar syrup. Sudden exposure to cold seems to increase the tendency to the disease; whilst when in warm comfortable quarters, they generally void their feces in a dry state in winter. Combs soiled by bees having dysentery should be washed by a small stream of water from a syringe, and may be returned to the bees in the Spring.

As in January, take care that all the necessary hives, tools, and implements are in readiness for summer.

MARCH.

This is the trying time on bees, and the seed time for the apiarian. Every hive should be examined, and if stores are scant, they should be supplemented. We cannot too strongly insist on the importance of *regular feeding*, if once begun. The feeders should be placed under the quilt, so that the bees can get at the *warm* liquid food, without leaving the cluster. They should not be fed in the morning for two reasons. First, Because it is apt to induce robbing; and, Secondly, Because when they have warm food during the day, bees are tempted to fly out, and many will thus be chilled. The auger feeder, described under "Feeding" answers well for this season of the year. The syrup should be made quite thin, as bees need much water. Early in March, or six weeks before fruit blossoms will appear, each colony should be confined, to only so many combs as it can well fill, by a movable division board until the combs are pretty well filled with brood, and at intervails of from five to ten days, the combs opened and an empty one inserted. By this means the heat of the colonies is retained, the queen stimulated, and brood reared very rapidly. Be cautious not to expand more rapidly than the increasing bees can fully cover the combs. The ventilation from above, should now be stopped and the quilts kept tightly packed, so as to retain the heat of the hive for rapid development. When there is abundant honey in sealed comb, bees are stimulated to use it by clipping off the caps and putting it in the broodnest. If there is sufficient honey in the combs no other feeding should be done at all, unless it is to be kept up regularly until the first blossoms appear. Guard carefully against robbing, by leaving no syrup or comb exposed, and by contracting the entrances, especially of weak stocks. If any hive is found queenless, it should be promptly united with some weak colony, and the combs preserved for use in the summer. It is a loosing business to attempt to keep a queenless colony. Before they can rear a queen they will almost certainly be lost from dwindling, robbing, or worms. But if united with a weak one, it makes it strong, and almost doubles its value. In the far North rye meal should be continued until flowers appear, but when wintered indoors we advise always to keep them in until the last of April or the first of May. If such colonies become uneasy, take them to their summer stands, (being careful to place each upon the site occupied the year before, to prevent confusion when they take their flight) and return them until the cold weather seems to be well over. Colonies wintered in the cellar are not prepared to stand the changes to which they are subject, if set out too early, and the result is great loss by "Spring Dwindling." Some bee-keepers advise setting such on their summer stands about the middle of this month and begin to feed artificial pollen. If stores are plentiful and sweet, such hives will go forward gradually with breeding in the cellar, and when warm weather begins to stir them, they are in much better condition than if set out earlier.

March or April is a good time to buy bees in old hives for transferring.

The selected stock should be strong in bees, with dark straight comb and *not* a last year's swarm, because in this is an old queen. One that has swarmed the preceeding year is much to be preferred as this has a young fertile queen.

If attention is given *regularly* to feeding small quantities of syrup every evening, from this time until flowers appear, you may expect large stocks and much honey. This is especially desirable when red raspberries are abundant.

APRIL.

This is the month in which bees need the most care. There are few sections in which honey is gathered, except in the far South, though bees are active bringing pollen, and raising young bees in abundance. In any locality it is important that the queen should be laying rapidly six weeeks before the fruit trees blossom, or before the first expected yield of honey.

During this month bees consume large quantities of honey in rearing brood. If stores are scant but few bees will be raised, and, perhaps, the abundant brood in the cells will be destroyed. Bees often starve at this season of the year, because the honey is consumed more rapidly than supposed. It is well to continue the operation of spreading the comb and inserting an empty one, or comb-foundation, every eight or ten days when the bees are doing well; being careful not to spread more rapidly than the increasing bees demand. If combs on hand are filled with sealed honey, clip the caps and place it in the centre. The bees will rapidly use and remove the honey, and the comb be appropriated to brood-rearing. Be careful to place no drone comb in the midst of the broodnest at this season, unless drones are desired very early for the purpose of Italianizing. If this is desired a sheet placed in the centre the first of this month, will give drone as early as swarming is generally desirable in the Middle States. This should be regulated by the climate. *Regular feeding*, with thin sugar syrup, about sunset during this month pays well, in additional stores later in the season. But even where the stocks are all strong and feeding deemed unnecessary, it is well to feed in the caps during any continued cold or rainy spell in this month and May.

In this month bees from the cellar should be set on the summer stands except far North, where, if they remain quiet, it may be best to wait until the first of May. This should be regulated by the season. They should be set out as soon as warm weather seems to have come and blossoms begin to appear. In setting out bees, open only a few stocks at a time, until the excitement of first flight is over. In the far north continue feeding rye and oat meal this month, so long as the bees will take it.

In the far South the swarming season is approaching and the directions for May and June are more appropriate. In the far North, March management applies. These notes apply more especially to the great middle section of the country. As bees are rapidly increasing during this month, common sense teaches us to take away absorbing material and cover the broodnest as closely as possible with warmer covering, so as to prevent upward ventilation and retain as much as possible of the animal heat of the hive. There is no danger of getting the hive too hot in this month, except in the far South. Sunshine on the hive stimulates them in spring. Wherever the wild cherry abounds it is best to give no room for storage of surplus honey from this source. Its honey is excellent for building up colonies, but unpleasantly bitter for table use.

At this season kill every worm or miller that may be seen. This saves trouble, as each one now rears four generations during summer.

Be careful in Spring, and then keep strong stocks, and the danger from worm is very small, especially if Italian or hybrid bees are kept. April and May are, perhaps, the best months for transferring. April in the South, and May farther North, when the first great brood rearing is over. If any queenless stocks still remain, unite them as recommended in March. Feeble colonies should be reinforced by a frame of hatching brood, placed in the centre, during this month. Do not cut away comb because it is dark or even mouldy. Mouldy or soiled comb can be easily renovated by water and the extractor. or with a strong syringe. Combs in which bees have died should be cleared of dead bees, even if it be necessary to scrape away a part of the cells on one or both sides of the comb.

MAY.

If care has been given as recommended, all stocks in mild latitudes should be crowded with brood in all stages of development. In the far North the stimulating of April is now in progress and in the Southern States the honey harvest is well begun. There the June management best applies to this month.

It seems to be the instinct of bees at this season to rear as much brood as possible. If any honey is to be gathered they bring it in rapidly. The more honey they get and the more they are fed the more rapidly they increase, provided the broodnest is not filled with it. If cold, windy, or rainy weather continue for several days, hives are very much checked in development and injured. Hence, under such circumstances, they should always be fed. Let the sun shine on the hives as much as possible during this month. Different management should be followed this month, if rapid increase of stocks is desired, instead of surplus honey.

If increase of stocks is the object much feeding is required, and new comb continually inserted to the capacity of ten or twelve frames, according to size. As soon as drones begin to hatch, by the middle or last of May. divide the strongest hive, by finding the queen and removing the comb to which she adheres and one or two more to a new hive, adding from two to four frames of artificial comb, according to the strength of the colony. Remove the old hive to a new locality and place the new one upon the old stand. The old one will rear a number of queen cells ready for insertion into other hives as swarms are made by either of the methods recommended under "Artificial Swarming." We would advise the above method or that of taking two combs from each of four hives and inserting empty ones in their places for beginners, giving each a queen cell, when made.

The novice should never attempt to more than double his colonies. He may expect the best results if he only makes one new swarm from each two, especially if he uses the extractor. We would advise getting an extractor, even though not more than two hives are kept.

These directions, concerning swarming, apply in many places to June, according to strength of colonies. If bees begin to "lay out" when the hives are crowded, they should be divided, the combs extracted, artificial foundation given, or honey boxes put on. Sometimes giving boxes will not set bees to work, and unless an extractor is at hand they should be divided. If surplus honey and not increase is sought, the extractor is almost essential. If it is freely used there is much less danger of swarming. Sometimes bees will take the swarming fever. If so, it is best to swarm them, raise young queens, as described above, and then reunite them with the young queens, giving ample surplus space in boxes at the top and sides, or by filling both the upper and lower chambers with combs, and foundation combs when the extractor is chiefly relied on.

In June we will give specific directions concerning putting on, and the management of boxes, which in middle latitudes where honey appears in abundance, should be used this month.

Hives with young queens are much more apt to make worker comb, if empty frames are given, than those with old queens, which make more drone comb. The best way to *prevent* swarming is by giving empty comb every few days, between two brood combs, by using the extractor freely on the combs in the broodnest, by giving ample surplus boxes, or by placing the hive above another having empty comb below, and closing all the entrances into the upper one, except through the lower. But if the swarming fever has once *begun* it cannot well be cured, except by dividing, after which they may be reunited.

If empty combs at any time are not in use, they should not be packed in a box, or moth eggs will soon hatch and destroy them. Hang them singly in a cool cellar or out building, where the air can pass around them and they are not apt to be injured.

JUNE.

In most sections in the North and Middle States this month is the great harvest time for the bee-keeper. It is also the great swarming season and every bee-keeper, who relies on natural swarming, must now keep constant watch over his bees.

Whenever bees are hived it is always well to put a card of honey and brood from the old stock into the hive. This will usually prevent the swarm from leaving the hive, and also furnish necessary supplies should a few days of cool, rainy weather immediately follow. For modes of hiving, and dividing artificially, see the chapter on this subject. There is always danger of hives becoming queenless after swarming, as the queen may be lost on her bridal tour, or fail to reach the right hive.

Such a queenless hive will soon become weak, and is liable to be destroyed by worms or robbers if not watched. Queenless stocks do not defend themselves as others. It is better to unite such stocks with others, unless queen-cells or young queens are at hand to give them, and afterwards divide again, if increase is desired. Be careful to remove drone combs from the brood nest that time and honey be not wasted in rearing too many. To prevent the swarming fever proceed as described in May, by using the extractor, doubling up, and exchanging combs ; or else give timely access to the honey boxes. At first only a small amount of surplus room should be given each hive. After the bees begin to work well in this, other boxes may be added. If starters of comb or comb foundation be placed in the boxes the bees will more readily commence on them.

At the commencement of a good honey flow at the last of May, or during this month each hive should have some surplus room if box honey is desired. As the season progresses, and the bees are rapidly working, these may be increased by removing and giving new boxes, by removing from the side to the top, or by lifting one tier of boxes and inserting another, according to the arrangement of the hive and the box prepared. Bees store faster in the lower chamber, and seal up the honey more quickly above. Where one has time, perhaps, the most profitable way to manage for honey is, to combine the use of the extractor and boxes. Build up rapidly in the spring, as described. Then in June—having the hive full of bees—contract the broodnest to six or eight frames—as many as the queen will keep full of brood. On each side place brood frames full of small boxes, hanging in the hives just as the regular frames. (See "Hives" and "Surplus Honey,") Two on each side are sufficient. If boxes larger than four and one half inches square are used, wire framed division boards, with proper openings, must be used between them and the broodnest. These frames can be constantly shifted, placing a full one above to be capped, moving out the inner one and inserting between it and the broodnest a frame filled with other boxes. As honey is rapidly stored in the broodnest, it may be extracted before it is capped over, the thickest and best drawn off from below and bottled, and the rest refed to the bees, to be stored in the boxes. This can be done to a great advantage during a honey drought, so as to keep the queen rapidly laying, and the stock strong for future work.

Where the extractor is used regularly it will be found much best to have a few extra combs, and as the combs to be extracted are removed replace them with others, and close up the hive. By keeping the frames in a carrying box, well covered they are exposed but a little time to robbers. If robbers abound they should be carried to a close barn or outer room and extracted. The best time for extracting is in the middle of the day, during a good honey harvest, when most of the old bees are absent in the fields. They will then scarcely notice the honey. Extract from two combs at a time. Clipp off the caps with a sharp knife, (see "Extractor") and hang them on opposite sides, close against the wire frame. Now turn the extractor a few moments until the honey is thrown from the sides next the wire cloth, and then turn the other sides of the combs to the wire cloth and turn as before. New combs, or those having in them pollen or brood should be turned very gently.

JULY.

Keep a constant watch for queenless colonies, and do not let them dwindle away. Prompt attention saves the colony. All the hives should be kept strong by regular feeding after sunset if pasturage fails. Care should be used at such times in opening hives. Always smoke the bees well before attempting it, and move gently, because bees are much more vicious when there is no honey in the fields. Keep boxes on and continue to extract according to the honey supply.

If small boxes are used in large frames they may be removed or exchanged with ease, just as the regular frames, by smoking the bees and then brushing them off with a green twig. When boxes are to be removed *too much* smoke will cause them to eat the caps from the honey. If section boxes, or any with more than one comb is used, it is often difficult to rid the boxes of bees when they are removed, and there is danger of losing the young bees by the method recommended, viz., putting into a box or barrel, and covering it with a sheet, which is turned over frequently as the escaping bees cluster upon it. A successful method is to have each hive numbered and as boxes are removed number them accordingly. Upon this place a corresponding box, with holes open between them, and lay them with the empty box uppermost in the honey house. The young bees will ascend into it. It is then closed and placed upon the hive from which the box is taken. This, however, is troublesome. The best way to remove them when honey is abundant and bees are gathering it rapidly, is to take off the boxes and set them by the hives in the evening. In the morning early the bees will be out, and they should then be removed.

Boxes should be watched for a few weeks after they are taken off. If the weather is warm and worms begin to hatch, they should be smoked with sulphur. It is most successfully used by heating a large piece of iron. Put it in an iron vessel and pour the flour of sulphur upon it. In this way there is no danger from fire. (See under "Honey Boxes.")

In sections where darker honey is gathered the last of this month, the nice white basswood, or clover honey comb should be promptly removed before it is soiled, or the white honey extracted before it is injured by admixture with the darker. During hot weather be careful always to give the broodnest good ventilation, but keep the boxes closed for wax working.

AUGUST.

In many places but little honey is gathered this month, but in others the main summer supply is laid away. Of course different management applies, according to location. If honey abounds, continue treatment as in July—keeping each hive supplied with boxes, or extracting frequently. Where dark buckwheat is plentiful we advise giving frames of foundation in exchange for sealed combs, which should be set away for winter. We advise this especially where bees can be gotten in the fall from neighbors who "take up" their bees and where aster, goldenrod, smartweed, or other fall flowers abound, which produce good honey. This can be saved and the less salable buckwheat honey be substituted for winter, or used for filling hives for bees gotten from neighbors.

This is the best month for Italianizing if it is done by purchasing queens, because they are cheaper than at any other time of the year; the hives are not necessarily disturbed during their previous work, and they go into winter quarters just right to turn out good Italian workers for the next season. Be careful always to have brood reared plentifully this month and next, even if feeding is necessary, because hives strong with young bees in the fall, winter much better, and develope much more rapidly in the spring than those that cease rearing brood at this season of the year. Whenever no good honey harvest is expected after this, care should be promptly taken to see that empty cells are in the centre of the hive for broodrearing, and that there is a full amount of supplies given for winter.

During the honey drought in this month, or whenever the bees cease to find honey in the fields, they are much more difficult to handle and much more given to robbing than at any other season. In opening or removing boxes be as gentle as possible, and always smoke well before opening a hive. Keep all stocks strong. If any seems weak build it up by inserting from one able to spare it, a comb or two of hatching brood. Keep the entrances contracted so as to prevent robbing. If it has fairly commenced stop it as recommended under "Robbing." Leave no sweets or bits of comb exposed.

If box honey is placed in a cool dry cellar there is less danger from hatching worms, and less yet if the combs are set on a shelf an inch or two apart, so as to permit the free circulation of air around them.

SEPTEMBER.

This month's operations are very important in preparing hives for winter. Unsealed late honey is generally poor winter food for bees. Hence if close extracting be continued late there is always danger, unless full sealed combs have been set away for them, or unless this be extracted and good sugar syrup be given as recommenced in the chapter on "Wintering." But where many fall flowers abound the main surplus of the year is sometimes gathered this month. Hence prompt attention should be given. To gather this fall honey the *extractor is almost invaluable*; for it will be not be stored in boxes when comb must be built anything like so rapidly as in the brood nest, which instinct teaches them must be filled now for winter.

This, like August, is a good time to introduce Italian queens or others in order to secure new brood, which is, as we believe, no less important with bees than other live stock.

Keep no queenless stocks beyond this month, unless queens are expected to be introduced, and in that case insert a comb or two of hatching brood from some that can spare them, in order to secure a supply of young bees for winter. Where little honey is gathered, the last of July and throughout August, but the fall harvest is good, the best time to divide bees is just after the summer harvest closes. By regular feeding during this time all the necessary queens may be reared, a good increase obtained, and the hives are all strong with bees to gather the fall honey and are also in the best condition for wintering.

In readjusting the comb for winter in this month or next, according to climate and honey flow, be careful always to give each hive a comb or two containing bee-bread, and in northern latitudes to cut a hole in each comb for winter passages, as recommended under "Wintering." Queens known to be old should always be replaced by young ones in the fall, even though you have to purchase the young queen. With a little care a supply of young queens may be easily kept on hand this time of the year. If feeding is necessary feed as rapidly as possible, unless it is desirable to stimulate broodrearing. Directions as to modes of shipping honey will be given next month.

In this month do not fail to contribute to, and carefully examine the bee department in your local and State fairs. You can there often get valuable information. But if there is no interest taken in this subject go to work and show its importance, and let the people know the great advantages of improved bee culture over old methods.

OCTOBER.

Except in the South complete all arrangements for winter early this month, and there where the honey flow ceases. See that each hive has proper absorbing material above, holes in the caps to give upward ventilation, the entrances contracted so as to keep out mice, and all snug for winter. Spare combs should be carefully preserved and laid away for use in the spring. Small and queenless colonies should be united, winter passages made, old queens superseded, and young ones introduced. Queens may be reared thus late by keeping one strong colony queenless, so that it will retain drones for fertilization.

Some stocks if not extracted may have too much honey. If so equalize them by exchanging with some poorer colony, and see that some empty comb is left near the bottom of the central frames for clustering. In modern climates sufficient passage is given from comb to comb for winter by laying a stick an inch in diameter across the frames, under the quilt, but in cold climates both this and holes in the comb are recommended. Remember that the essentials of good wintering are, a plenty of young bees with a fertile queen, an abundance of good sealed honey easily accessible, and warmth with proper ventilation.

A good cotton quilt with three or four thicknesses of batting, makes perhaps, as good as any obsorbing material, It is light and may be easily removed for feeding or for examination.

To unite bees smoke them thoroughly and sprinkle them with sweetened water, strongly scented with anise or peppermint, and either shake the bees altogether into an empty box, using as many of the best combs as are necessary in the new hive, and then pour the bees at the entrance of the hive, or after smoking and sprinkling well put one frame alternately from each hive into the new hive, brushing all the bees off at the extrance and set this new hive in an intermediate position between the two.

If any boxes have remained on till this month they should be now removed and packed as neatly as possible in crates with glass sides, as recommended under the head of "Crates." If your honey is extracted drain off any thin honey on the top of your jar or bottle. Seal it up neatly, labeling it with your *name, apiary*, and *kind of honey*, and then sell as conveniently to your own home as you can to advantage. It is always well to let the people know the superiority of honey gathered by improved methods so as to build up a local trade and increase consumption. Boxes of comb honey should be packed rather tight in crates. In making large shipments it is best to attend the car to see that they are handled safely. Small amounts may be sent securely in shipping boxes in which the crates are supported on small wire coil springs or rubber tubing.

NOVEMBER.

The honey season is now over, and all the hives should have been prepared for winter, but if a few have been neglected they may be so prepared on some warm day in this month. If hives are to be taken indoors they should not be carried in before the cold weather has set in in earnest, or it may be necessary to return them to their summer stands because of uneasiness. The later they are housed the better, provided the weather continues open, so that the bees can fly and void their feces. It is better to take them in the day after they have flown freely. Before cold weather sets in, colonies to be wintered on summer stands, should be packed with absorbing material, and given upward ventilation through it.

In the far South some parts of October management best suits this month. Unite all weak stocks after smoking well, as recommended last month. They will not fight much now when united. See that all unused hives or implements are carefully housed for the winter.

DECEMBER.

This should be a month of repose with the bees. Less brood is reared in November and December than in any other part of the year. Now is the time to study the bee business, prepare hives, crates and boxes, and all necessary implements. Decide with regard to setting out shade trees for their honey qualities, orchards, and cultivation of honey crops so as to be able to secure seed or young trees for planting when the time comes. See that hives are protected from cold winds, and occasionally clear the dead bees from the bottom board. As in January, keep the bees quiet as possible.

We would advise beginners especially to study carefully this Monthly Management, and use practical good sense in following it, according to climate, the particular season, and the honey flow at the time. In bee-keeping it is of the first importance that the right thing be done at the right time.

CHAPTER LX.

HIVES.

The value of a hive depends upon its size, shape, and the advantages secured in its construction.

SIZE.

Experience has demonstrated that, as a general rule, when we vary from the correct size, the larger the hive the fewer swarms we get, and the smaller the hive, the smaller the swarms will be, and the greater the danger of over-swarming. A hive should contain about two thousand cubic inches, in the clear. A stock in a hive of this size, will swarm more regularly than from a larger one, and store more surplus honey. While, if the hive be much smaller, the colony will often fail to lay up provisions enough for our long winters. All the hives should be made of the same size, as a very large swarm will usually be no larger, after a few months, than one of medium size, while a small swarm may be as large as any at the end of the season, much depending upon its having a prolific queen, good weather and abundant pasturage.

SHAPE.

Upon the shape of the hive, depends the economy of heat for breeding, and safety in wintering. If a hive of proper size be too high, less box honey is obtained; but if too shallow, it not only takes more workers to cover the lower part of the combs, to protect them from the moth, and keep up the required heat for breeding, but the winter stores are scattered over so large a surface, and of so little depth, that although the heat arising from the swarm will keep the honey warm directly above the bees, they soon consume that to the top of the hive. When this happens in very cold weather, if there are no holes through the combs, the bees die of starvation, as it is certain death for them to venture around the edge of the frosty combs by which they are surrounded. Hence, swarms often perish with ample stores in the hive. For these evident reasons, we would recommend that frames be long and shallow in warm climates, and deeper and shorter according to climate, approximating to a square where it becomes very cold.

More box honey can be secured with shallow frames, both because there is more surface for boxes, and because bees store more readily near the broodnest. But this advantage is counterbalanced in cold climates by the greater depth for wintering, the greater ease of extracting, and the greater depth for boxes beside the broodnest when shorter and deeper frames are used.

"THE ADVANTAGES SECURED IN THE CONSTRUCTION OF HIVES."

Centuries ago, intelligent men were convinced that, if *complete control of the bees and combs* could be obtained, bee-keeping must become a sure and systematized business, both pleasant and profitable. The practice of murdering whole colonies, with the brimstone match, for their stores, was gradually abandoned by the introduction of surplus honey boxes, with glass sides in which the bees would store their tempting sweets in the most beautiful and marketable form. Yet bee culture still bore the stigma of a business of "*luck and chance,*" or *working in the dark*, and all attempts at improvement were failures, as there were no facilities for examining the interior of the hive to learn the cause of or apply a remedy for any defect that might there exist. But "necessity is the mother of invention." This darkness was first gradually dispelled, in Europe, by the invention of a movable-comb hive, called the "Leaf Hive," by Francis Huber, of Geneva, as early as 1795.

It had long been known, that bees would start and build their combs with considerable regularity from strips placed across the top of the hive, by which the combs could be lifted out by cutting loose their side attachments from the hive. These "bars" led to "bar frames," which are most briefly described in Mr. Langstroth's Patent, referred to in note on page 140, in which he shows that he is the inventor of the shallow chamber and some other features connected therewith, which will be understood by the descriptions which he gives of previous inventions, which we abbreviate as follows: The Huber frame consisted of sections, the top and side bars fitting close together, with no honey receptacles above, but the necessity of cutting the side attachments of the comb was obviated.

9. Taylor's Frame.

W. Augustus Munn, Esq., invented the "bar and frame hive," and published a description of it in London, in 1844. In 1851, he published a second edition of his pamphlet, in which, describing his "improved hive," he says he has "very materially

HIVES.

simplified the construction of the bar and frame hive, by forming the oblong bar-frames into triangular frames, and making them *lift out at the top* instead of the back of the bee-box." M. Debeauvoy published the second edition of his "Guide del Apiculteur," as early as 1847, in which he describes his movable frames with narrow tops and side bars, the tops fitting closely to the honey-board above, and the sides to the walls of the hive. In 1851, he published his third edition in Paris, in which he describes his new frames, having their sides at suitable distances from the bottom and walls of the hive, with the tops fitting closely together, but still in connection with a honey-board above the top bars. Thus, movable-comb frames were much improved and used in many parts of Europe, by Huber, Debeauvoy, Munn, Taylor, Bevan, Golding, Huish, Dzierzon and others, while the "brimstone match" bore sway in America. But, the key to successful bee-keeping once found, nothing could stop its progress. The bounds of the Atlantic were passed, and many in our country became acquainted with Huber's "Leaf Hive" and movable-comb system.

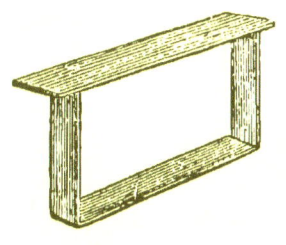

10. Oblong Munn Frame.

HIVE ESSENTIALS.

There are now made many good movable comb hives among which the beginner should make choice, and have *all the hives in the apiary made just alike,* so that any frame or any part of a hive will fit any other hive. Exact workmanship is of the first importance. There is now no patent on any important part of movable comb hives, and any person can make plain wooden ones as he desires. Perhaps the best way is for each beginner, if unable to make his own hives and boxes, to get such good hives as are manufactured most convenient to him, and at the best rates from good lumber.

We recommend simple stands made of a bottom board the width of the hive and four or five inches longer for an alighting board. This should be nailed to 2x4 inch strips so as to place the hives near the ground. The hive should be hinged on the back end of this, to be raised for cleaning off the bottom board. The frames should hang on metal stips one-fourth of an inch above the edge of the rabbits to prevent killing bees when handling them, and also to prevent the ends of the frames from being glued down too tightly with propolis. The alighting board should slant from the front, that overladen bees may crawl in when blown down by the wind.

We recommend that the cap be of the same frame dimensions as the body of the hive so as to be used as a double hive—with two tiers of frames for extracting if desired. The top should be one solid board with good cleats underneath, or if made of two pieces the boards should be well seasoned and tongued and groved and glued to prevent leaking.

Formerly honey boards were used above the frames to hold surplus boxes, but they are difficult to make and not so convenient as quilts. These should be made from a simple sheet of ducking or other firm material in which the bees will not gnaw holes. They should be a little larger than the space to be covered, so as to tuck down well and cover the bees, and the cloth be well shrunk before making, lest they become too small after using for a time. They should be hemmed and in the centre of each a small hole for feeding, covered with a flap, which is raised only when needed. Honey boxes may be set directly on the tops of the frames, or better upon strips resting on the frames, and the quilt tucked around them to keep in the heat. When sections are used in wide frames they should be closed at the side with a follower which may be tied or held in place by a foot piece which prevents its falling over. Perhaps the best way to manage boxes is to place them in wide two inch frames. These may be either of the dimensions of the regular frame or half the depth so as to hold only one row of small boxes. Two tiers of the latter are used at the sides of the broodnest and one or two above, as desired or as seems necessary. (See "Honey Boxes," p. 56.)

These wide frames which hold the honey boxes of the same width have on one side strips of tin wide enough to leave passages for the bees at the bottom and top into the honey boxes of one-fourth to three-eights of an inch. By this means the comb is secured accurately in boxes which may afterwards be covered with glass or not, as prefered and packed uniformly in crates to suit the market.

Two close fitting division boards should belong to each hive for contracting it when necessary and to be used in packing for winter. When not needed below they can be hung in the upper box. Narrow strips of heavy wood having one end cut diagonally make excellent entrance blocks.

The bee-keeper should make his hives during winter when not pressed with work, and have a full supply of boxes, and crates, or barrels on hand when the honey season opens. It is too late to make them when the bees begin to need attention. Success depends greatly in providence for the busy time, and prompt attention when demanded in the apiary.

PAINTING AND CLOUDING HIVES.

Hives should be painted as soon as made, and three or four weeks before being used, as the smell of fresh paint is offensive to the bees. They may be painted every shade of color, for the sake of variety, but red is most apt to be noticed from a distance, while white or clouded looks best near by. To cloud a hive, paint it white, and while the last coat is fresh, place the hive in a horizontal position, passing under it the smoke and blaze of a lamp with a small round wick. If the clouding be done in a room out of the wind, with a little practice the hives may be made to resemble marble, and are very ornamental, although it costs nothing for material, and can be done in five minutes.

OBSERVING HIVES.

Nearly all of the facts in the physiology of the honey bee may be tested by having a glass hive, with a single comb taken from a full hive in the parlor, office or sitting room. If more than one comb is used some of the operations will be hid and the queen will often be between them and invisible. Observing hives are of little use with more than one frame. The bottom should be made of thick board four inches wide Bore a hole in one end of this, so as to open up into the hive and make a small ventilator, and cover it with wire cloth. The two sides should be of glass, two inches apart, sliding into rabbets in the ends. The queen may be seen depositing eggs in such a hive, without danger, and if a comb with eggs, brood, and bees from an ordinary hive be given, the whole operation of forming queen cells, and rearing queens can be seen. The bottom board should extend three or four inches in front, so that the bees enter from without the room.

THE CIRCULAR SAW.

One of the absolute necessities about the apiary is a circular saw. It may be run by foot power if the number of colonies is small, but for over twenty colonies, some other power will be required. Unless one is

THE CIRCULAR SAW.

in the business pretty extensively he can buy the section frames more cheaply than he can make them, but even when these are bought, the saw is indispensible for cutting out frames, hives, and the multitude of small pieces that are constantly needed. The saw being so useful, in this section, we propose to give some directions for managing it so as to have it work satisfactorily.

In the first place it is necessary that the saw should be perfectly round. It should be screwed on to the mandrel, and a mark put on both, so that always afterward it may be replaced in exactly the same position, if it is ever required to be removed. Now, the mandrel should be placed in its bearings, and the belt put on, so that it may be just tight enough not to slip. Next an emery wheel should be laid upon the table over the saw slot, and then the table must be lowered until just the points of any teeth that may be longer than others will touch as the saw is turned. The saw must be run and the table lowered gradually till every tooth touches, when the saw will be round. The emery stone will not be injured, nor will the saw either, even if some teeth are ground off blunt. The point does the cutting, and if that is sharp, it does not matter how broad the tooth is. Next the saw is to be filed. The ripper can be filed best with a cant file. [See cut Fig. 1.] Large enough to fit the teeth

FIG. 1.

of the saw, which by the way, must be as small for the size of the saw as they are ever made. The cross-cut, is filed with the ordinary three-cornered file. The filing must be done entirely on the under side of the tooth, and should not be continued after the point is sharp. The under side of each tooth of the ripper should have the direction of a tangent to a circle of half the diameter of the saw, and if the cross-cut of one-third the diameter. Fig. 2 will illustrate the meaning. The teeth on the left are correctly filed, the others incorrectly. The teeth may be filed slightly flairing by holding the file obliquely, especially of the cross-cut, as they are to be used generally in soft wood. The next operation is setting. This may be done with the ordinary saw-set,

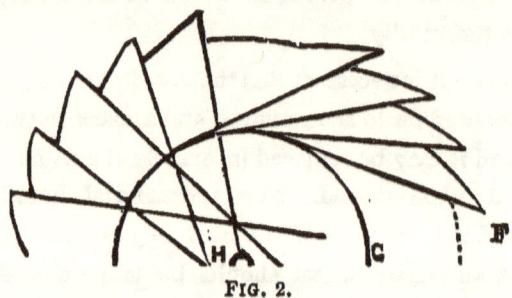

FIG. 2.

made much like a knife with notches of different widths along the edge for bending the teeth; but a beginner will generally succeed best with one of the various patent affairs containing a gauge. Whatever is used the set must be as little as possible—just bending the point of the teeth outside the plane of the saw as in Fig. 3. So that the end of the kerf is

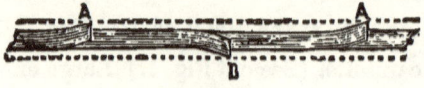

FIG. 3.

square across, and not containing a point in the middle, as in Fig. 4.

FIG. 4.

However carefully the saw may be set, the teeth will probably not all get exactly the same amount of bending; so to make them perfectly even the saw must next be jointed. This is done by turning it backward and holding an oil stone first against one side and then the other. Next the saw is to be tried, to see if it is just right. It ought now to cut rapidly, straight and smoothly—every cut a glue joint. If it does not run straight—either drawing the board away from the gauge or wedging it so tightly as to stop—the trouble is either with the saw or the guage. Look at the end of the saw kerf, if it is pointed on one side or the other, the teeth on the pointed side are too long, and they must be filed again and thus shortened. If the kerf is square across, the trouble is with the guage. It must be made exactly parallel with the saw. If the further end is nearer the saw than the other, the piece will wedge; if nearer, the work can not be held close to the guage. The table should be raised so that the teeth just reach through the piece sawed.

There ought to be a pretty heavy fly wheel connected with the saw, and as much difference between the size of the driving wheel and the pully of the mandrel as convenient, so as to obtain as much speed as possible; But any arrangement of geared wheels to obtain speed is not satisfactory.

FOUL BROOD.

This is a disease which, as its name indicates, attacks the *brood*, and soon destroys a colony by preventing any brood from coming to maturity. We are thankful that personally we know nothing of this disease. Those who have suffered from it pronounce it very fatal, though there seems to be several phases of the disease; some far more fatal than others. The disease is contagious, like small pox or cholera and like these is propagated by very small spores or germs, which attack brood and destroy it. To check or cure this disease the fungus growth must be destroyed.

Salicylic acid has, by experiment in Germany been found to be destructive to this foreign growth, if properly applied. Yet some, among whom is John Hunter, state that it has failed with them in effecting a cure.

From what we have been able to learn of the disease, we believe that the ordinary type may be cured by the application of the acid as recommended by Mr. Muth, of Cincinnati, as follows: Make a solution of 128 grains of salicylic acid, 128 grains soda borax, 16 ounces of water, [distilled preferred.] Spray this solution on the combs containing brood, after uncapping cells that are sealed. The solution does not injure the bees, but seems to kill the spores of the disease. The spores find their way into the honey and the disease is spread among bees that eat of the honey from an affected hive. Doubtless robber bees help to scatter the disease. It is well in severe cases to remove the bees from the honey for three or four days and then place them in another hive. Remove all affected combs to a single hive. If possible remove the queen, and the bees will clear out the combs. If it is desirable, sprinkle a second time with the salicylic acid mixture. But in case the disease seems to be of a very malignant type it may be best, if this remedy fails, and the bees deprived of their queen do not clean up the comb, to drive out the bees and after three or four days put them into new hives, and then use the heroic treatment; burying all the affected combs and thoroughly washing the hives with some disinfectant before being used.

FERTILIZATION IN CONFINEMENT.

As queens are fertilized on the wing, every person who has reared Italian queens knows the difficulty of getting them purely mated, as they often meet black drones from distant apiaries. This trouble interferes much with the business of queen rearing, since the bee master must wait several weeks to test the purity of a queen before sending her out, or else sell merely as a fertile queen, at a reduced price. The desirability of fertilization in confinement, so as to be certain of purity, has been long felt, but has until recently been considered impossible, and even now some are too incredulous to accept a fact, *"because I have not done it."*

Mrs. Tupper announced her success at artificial fertilization some years ago, but being pressed by business cares—almost broken hearted—and besides ridiculed for her statements, she did not fully carry out her experiments. She communicated her experience to others, who also reported success in a number of cases, when the proper conditions were secured.

Mr. Jno. F. Lafferty, of Illinois, states that he has many times succeeded in sending out queens to mate by giving light on a bright day, when she is two or three days old. The trouble in all attempts at artificial fertilization seems to be in ascertaining just when the queen is ready to meet the drone.

Many things indicate that the subject is about meeting with a successful solution. One of our progressive appiarians informs me that he has this year succeeded, not only in fertilizing his queens in confinement, but also in selecting the drone with which they shall mate. He has described to us the process which is very simple and practicable, but as he is already booked for a paper on "Fertilization in Confinement" at the National Convention, in October next, he will then make known his system to the public. So much progress has been made in seemingly impossible matters, it seems strange that lovers of the art would, by untimely derision, check needed experiments and progress.

CHAPTER X.

BIOGRAPHY OF BEE-KEEPERS.

Believing it a subject of interest to most bee-keepers, we devote this chapter to a brief sketch of several persons whose labors have helped to advance the cause of apistic science in modern times.

Foremost of all stands Francis Huber, who was born at Geneva, in 1750. He is noted for many wonderful experiments and discoveries in the natural history, physical economy, and habits of the honey bee. By nature a clear and close observer, he was so assiduous in his duties that he lost his eye sight in early life. But nothing daunted, with wonderful perseverance, he continued his researches, using the eyes of his faithful servant, Francis Bernens, for making observations. In 1795 he invented and used his Leaf Hive, which consisted of eight close fitting sections or frames, opening out on hinges, like the leaves of a book. (Doubtless his idea of combs in sections was derived from the observation hives used by naturalists in his day, and improvements on the Grecian hive having top bars and comb guides as described by Abbe Della Recca, in his publication, in Paris, in 1790).

The results of Huber's experiments may be summed up under four heads:

First. *As to Eggs.*—That the queen lays two kinds of eggs. One kind

BIOGRAPHY OF BEE-KEEPERS.

FRANCIS HUBER.

—unfecundated—which produces males or drones. The other—fertilized—which produces workers, and these—when developed with royal jelly in queen cells—produce perfect females or queens.

Second. *As to Queens.*—That they are the only *perfect* females; that they leave the hive early in life to meet the drones on the wing; that they are incapable of fertilization after the third week of life, and ever after lay only drone eggs; that one impregnation lasts for life, after which they lay eggs regularly arranged in the comb, one egg in each cell; that workers which have been partially fed on royal jelly sometimes lay eggs, but irregularly and only such as produce drones. He exploded the idea that workers were neuters, proving them to be undeveloped females.

Third. *As to Pollen.*—That pollen is the natural food of young bees or larvæ, when prepared by the nursing bees; that without it brood cannot be reared, and that honey is the chief food of the mature bees.

Fourth. That wax is a secretion from the body of the bee, and not gathered as previously supposed. That it is made chiefly from the saccharine part of honey.

As his views were received and adopted, others were led to improve on the Leaf Hive. First, by changing the shape of the edges to prevent the destruction of bees in shutting the leaves, then by arrangements for elevating one frame at a time into a glass case for examination, then by using the simple bar, after the Grecian method, lifted from the top of the hive. Then with bar and frames on the principle of a hive within a hive modified and improved as found to-day among apiarians.

Naturally bars led to frames. Huber obviated the necessity of cutting the comb loose by having it built in sections of the hive. But for practical reasons the bar and frame was soon used within boxes answering the same purpose.

Henry Taylor, whose "Manual of Bee-keeping" was first published in 1838, describes a frame like the cut on page 197, in which uprights were used inside the hive to prevent bees from attaching combs to the hive.

Major William Augustus Munn, so well known as the author of the revised edition of Dr. Bevan's book on the honey bee, as early as 1844, described his box with oblong bar and frame. He invented it in 1834, at twenty-four years of age, and after nine years of trial took out letters patent in Paris, in 1843. This was for a box and frame similar to those now in use. (See page 198.) In 1844 he described them fully in a pamphlet published in London, and in 1851 it was fully exhibited at the great fair in London. In 1852 Mr. Langstroth took out letters patent in America, somewhat simplyfying the same principles. About the same time Dzierzon, in Germany invented his new hive. Each seemingly independent of the other adopted similar hives.

Major Munn was a genial, hospitable English gentleman of intelligence. Being an enthusiast on bee-culture, he spent much time in studying the nature and habits of bess. Like Quinby he wrote much on the subject for agricultural and other papers. His most lasting work is the revised edition of Dr. Bevan's great work on the honey bee—the most scientific work ever written on bees in England.

Robert Huish, who published his book on bees in 1840 and 1844, was a man of the highest culture and ability, a member of the Academy of Arts and Sciences, at Gollingen, and honorary member of the Natural Institute of France. He seemed to have loved bees and bee-culture, but his work is interesting chiefly as illustrating the folly of theories not based on close observation. His book seems to have been written mainly to attack Huber and his theories. It shows how truth alone will survive

COPYRIGHT, 1875, BY J. H. NELLIS & BRO., PUBLISHERS, CANAJOHARIE, N.Y.

Yours respectfully,
M. Quinby

while attacks upon it must suffer. Among English apiarians Golding, Hunter, Neighbor, Pettit and Cotton deserve favorable mention.

Moses Quinby, of New York, was eminently practical in his efforts and writings; the direct aim of which was to raise bee-keeping to the dignity of a distinct and successful business pursuit. His "Mysteries of Bee-keeping" is the result of twenty years of careful observation and practice, suggested and guided by Dr. Bevan's book. It was first published in 1853, almost simultaneous with Mr. Langstroth's book, and what seemed remarkable at the time, they agreed on almost all the wondrous facts concerning bees, so much at variance with the received notions. This book, with its revised edition of 1865, was eminently practical, carrying it even to a fault. His mode of management for common box hives was beneficial in its day; but now, when all progressive bee-keepers want the movable comb hives, this becomes a great fault in the book. The amount of quiet work done by him gratuitously in receiving and instructing visitors, in answering letters and enquiries, besides regular contributions to the press on his favorite subject, is amazing. A man of genial presence, of kind and generous impulses, and possessed of true kindness of heart; he is much missed by bee-keepers of our land, and especially by those of his native State, who looked to him as their leader and guide. Many regret that he was not spared to complete a work which he contemplated on advanced bee-culture. The Quinby Hive, though extreme in size, was most successful under his management. He is especially known as the inventor of the Quinby Smoker, by his practical writings, by his peculiar hive, and by the theory—not fully accepted by many—that under proper favorable circumstances the liquid part of honey may be entirely evaporated in the body of the bee.

The name of Rev. L. L. Langstroth is a household word with every advanced apiarian: He was among the first to introduce movable comb

REV. L. L. LANGSTROTH.

hives into America, taking out letters patent in 1852 for the hive that still bears his name. It embodies the oblong frame of Major Munn, and the box of Dr. Bevan. Involving the same principles it is decidedly an improvement in mechanical construction upon those in use in England. Mr. Langstroth deserves, and rightly receives, great credit for his persevering efforts and experiments in his chosen pursuit, for an abundance of pioneer work, for his zeal in introducing Italian bees, and improvements for doing so. But his book on the "Honey Bee" is the crowning work of his life, and a contribution to apistic science, which will continue to live. It lacks the practical character of Quinby's work, but is far superior in scientific accuracy and beauty of expression to any American work which has yet appeared, or probably will appear, because henceforth the demand is for something more practical.

H. A. King has, perhaps, done more than any other man in America in calling the attention of the masses to the importance of improved bee-culture. His American Hive, in its different forms, has, we think, been used more extensively than any other. The *Bee-keepers Journal* commenced in 1868, with a circulation of two thousand copies, at one time ran up to near thirty thousand. "Hints to Bee-keepers" ran up to thirty thousand copies, and of the old "Bee-keepers' Text Book" up to the present time there has been sold about fifty-one thousand copies. This work, however, was largely the production of N. H. King, deceased, who was one of the real pioneers of scientific bee-keeping, and to him the intensely practical character of this book is due.

In 1874 H. A. King, in connection with ourself commenced the publication of the *Bee-Keepers' Magazine*, and in 1875 he retired permanently from the bee-business to engage more fully in preaching the Gospel and in the dissemination of religious literature.

REV. H. A. KING.

Baron Von Berlepsch at first violently opposed the theories of Dzierzon, but having by experiment proven their truth, he became their warmest advocate. His name is associated with his movable frame hive in Germany, which was suggested to him on seeing that used by Dzierzon, in 1838. It was invented and used from 1840 to 1845, when he greatly improved it by leaving space between the frames and the walls of the

BARON VON BERLEPSCH.

hive, to prevent the bees from gluing them fast. They were in all respects the same as the majority of frames now in use, and above the frames this hive had an air space, and above this, a perforated top with surplus honey receptacles. He used this till 1850, when he added side projections to the frames, and described the same in the *Bienen-*

CAPTAIN T. E. VON SIEBOLD.

Zeitung, for May 1852. It has been adopted as the standard hive by the Italian bee-keepers.

Being a man of wealth and leisure he gave much attention to his favorite subject. His last book on bee culture is said to be one of the most complete ever written.

He invited Captain T. E. Von Siebold, professor of zoology and anatomy in the University of Munich, to his apiary to test by experiment the theories of Dzierzon, and especially those connected with the parthenogenesis of the queen. He found on examination that the parts adhering to a young queen returning to her hive from her bridal tour were identical with the male organs of the drone; that the spermatheca of the queen was filled with the seminal fluid of the drone, and that worker eggs were accompanied with spermatozoa. Prof. Leuckart, at the request of Baron Berlepsch dissected a drone laying queen, and found no semen in the spemathaca, In 1852 Dr. Jos. Leidy, of Philadelphia, dissected a queen for Mr. Langstroth, with the same results as with Siebold. These two facts prove the correctness of Dzierzon's theory, since eggs of unfertilized queens do undoubtedly hatch and produce drones.

In closing this sketch we must not omit to mention the German apiarian Von Hrushka, the inventor of the Honey Extractor, to which we are, in American bee-keeping, so greatly indebted. In the apiary it is second to none of the important discoveries, in practical utility.

Few men have taken a deeper interest in the pioneer work of bee-culture than Mr. W. W. Cary, of Colerain, Massachusetts. About the year 1850 he made the acquaintance of Mr. Langstroth, then living at Greenfield, Mass, and spent some time with him experimenting with hives and bees. The greatest confidence and friendship has always existed between them. Hearing in 1860 of the successful importation of

PROF. LEUCKART.

a few Italian bees by Mr. Samuel B. Parsons, of Flushing, New York, Mr. Cary visited him and spent the summer with him in rearing and experimenting with Italian bees. Since then he has labored to disseminate this bee in purity.

After one failure Mr. Cary succeeded in procuring a colony of Egyp-

W. W. CARY.

tian bees, but finding them inferior to the Italians, he abandoned them without an attempt to sell.

Though sixty-four years of age he is still much interested in the introduction of new races of bees and in furthering in all honorable ways improvements in bee-culture.

Mrs. Ellen S. Tupper has most satisfactorily proven that women may successfully follow this new business. With great industry and perseverance she maintained and educated her large family mainly by bee-keeping. A close observer and pithy writer, she has done much to attract attention to this industry. Misfortunes, however, have followed her. At one time her apiary was destroyed by a hurricane. A few years afterwards her house was burned in winter, which involved the loss also of all her bees, as they were wintering in the cellar. Heart-broken and almost, if not quite, demented by losses and physical prostration, other troubles thickened around her, but she is again recovering physically, mentally, and pecuniarily. She has again gathered an apiary, and with a woman's perseverance amid trials, comes forward again with her pen to help the cause she loves. It was Mrs. Tupper who first announced success in artificial fertilization of queens. Though pronounced impossible her statement is verified by recent experiments.

Foremost among German apiarians stands Dzierzon, a Roman Catholic Priest, of Carlesmarkt, in Silesia. In 1838 he adopted a hive with movable bars alone, which was afterward greatly improved. He first discovered that bees will take flour instead of pollen in spring, and introduced its use, but he is best know as the author of the theory of the "Parthenogenesis of the Queen," so long derided, but now thoroughly established and accepted. His improvements and remarkable success in bee-culture attracted great attention throughout Germany and rapidly created a revolution in German bee-keeping.

Rev. E. Van Slyke is well known to the readers of the bee journals of America, as a scientific apiarist of the most progressive school. He commenced in New York City, in 1867, the publication of the *American Bee Gazette*. It was through its foreign columns that American bee-keepers first became acquainted with the honey extractor

BOIGRAPHY OF BEE-KEEPERS.

REV. FATHER DZIERZON

of Von Hruschka. Two articles on that subject published in two successive numbers, were hailed with delight and apparent sensation throughout the United States. When Mr. Samuel Wagner, after the late war of the rebellion, resumed the publication of fhe *American Bee Journal*, a movement was made for consolidation, which resulted in the union of the *Gazette* and *Journal* and afterwards appeared in Washington, D. C., under the name of *American Bee Journal and Gazette*. Mr. Van Slyke never dealt harshly with the supposed discoverer of new facts in his favorite pursuit, but patiently put them to the test of practical experiment, and so soon as demonstrated to his satisfaction, gave them to the people through the journals of the country. He was an ardent advocate of the truth of Mrs. Tupper's discovery of the posibility of fertilizing queen bees in confinement, now so fully demonstrated, and practised by Prof. Hasbrouck.

Before closing this sketch of those who have rendered valuable service to apistic science by their writings or other labors, we would not fail to make honorable mention of J. S. Harbison, Adair, Dr. Metcalf, Prof. A. J. Cook, Mr. A. I. Root, Mr. T. G. Newman, all of whom have added largely to the modern literature of this subject. While Harbison and Root, with J. E. Hetherington, Adam Grimm, Doolittle, Nellis, Clark, Hosmer, C. J. Quinby, T. F. Bingham, and a host of others, whose names our limits forbid mention, but whose faithful labors are worthy of all praise, have demonstrated, in the shape of tons of honey, the entire correctness of the new theories of successful bee management, and to whom we still look for yet new discoveries in this fruitful field

In mentioning names we make no invidious distinction, but urge all to activity in developing the rich honey resources of our land as they reveal themselves in the blooming flowers.

REV. E. VAN SLYKE.

THE BEE-KEEPERS' MAGAZINE.

An Illustrated Monthly Journal of 32 octavo pages, devoted entirely to scientific and practical bee-keeping.

Its contributors are the best and most experienced bee-keepers of the United States. Large space is devoted to beginners, giving useful information just when it is most needed throughout the year.

TERMS.—$1.50 a year, in advance. Subscriptions may commence at any time.

The New Bee-Keepers' Text Book.

CLOTH, post-paid, ...	$1.00.
IN PAPER COVERS, post-paid, . .	75 cts.

The BEE-KEEPERS' TEXT BOOK, of which there have been sold nearly fifty-three thousand copies, has done more than all others combined to bring to the attention of the masses the importance of rational bee-keeping as a pleasant and profitable life pursuit, and now that the book has been thoroughly revised, largely rewritten, finely illustrated, and brought up to the present advanced stages of bee-keeping, it is hoped that the new book may speedily obtain a wider circulation than that reached by the old.

☞ AGENTS WANTED!
LARGE CASH COMMISSION.

Agents canvassing for the MAGAZINE can very profitably handle this Book. We keep on sale all other books on bee-keeping, at publishers' prices. Address,

ORANGE JUDD CO,	Or,	A. J. KING & CO,
245 Broadway,		61 Hudson St.,
NEW YORK.		NEW YORK.

PRICE LIST

OF

APIARIAN SUPPLIES

A. J. KING & CO., 61 Hudson St., N. Y.

OR,

ORANGE JUDD CO., 245 Broadway, N. Y.

TERMS:—CASH.

MOTTO:—First-class goods, quick sales and small profits, and promptness in filling orders.

REQUIREMENTS:—Name, Post Office, County and State. Also, if not to go by mail, Express or Freight Office, County and State All to be written very plainly.

N. B. The goods offered in this List are manufactured under our direct supervision, and of the best materials, and are first-class in every respect. The bee-hives are painted with two coats of white lead, and are provided with full sets of frames and surplus honey sections.

NEW AMERICAN BEE-HIVE:

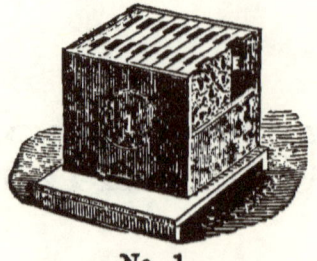

No. 1.

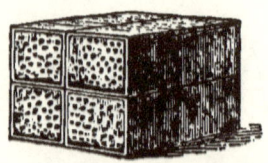

No. 2.

No. 1 represents the main body or breeding apartment. No. 2 represents the double tier of four honey-boxes, each one of which is composed of seven two pound sections. This hive contains nine regular 12x12 American frames. The cover (not shown in the engraving) is arranged so as to slip down over the body of the hive, making a double wall for wintering. It also reduces the bulk of the hive so much that the railroad companies charge but one-half the usual freight rates. The double tier of boxes fit exactly inside the brood frames, and when the cover is slipped down, it is almost as compact as when shipped as material.

1 complete Hive, with all accompaniments....................$4 00
5 to 20 complete Hives, with all accompaniments,.............. 3 50
Material (except glass) in lots of five or more, each.............. 2 25

These two styles of hives (American Eclectic) are deservedly the most popular of any in the market, and are both adapted for either extracted or box honey and double width frames filled with surplus boxes may be used in the breeding departments as well as in any other hives.

We also furnish finished hives of

ALL THE OTHER LEADING STYLES,

or materials for the same (in lots of five hives each), at lowest rates. Prices furnished on application.

ECLECTIC BEE-HIVE.

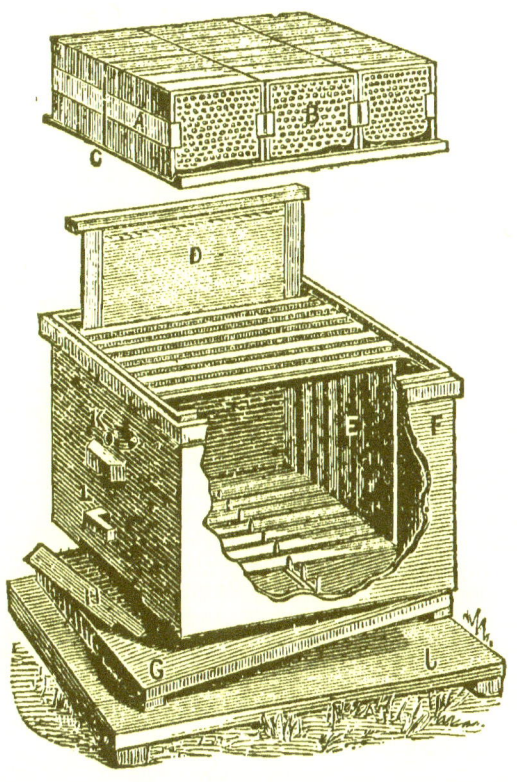

The above cut represents the Eclectic Bee Hive (except the cap) with one end cut away to show the inside arrangement. *J*, the stand ; *G*, bottom board of hive, hinged at the back, with hive raised up a little to show ease of cleaning bottom board ; *H*, slide to contract or close entrance ; *L*, button to hold slide in place ; *K*, upper entrance ; *E*, movable frames, supported on smooth iron metal rest for top bars, and separated at bottom by metal spacer, which is attached to each side of bottom of hive three-eight inch above bottom board to prevent crushing bees ; *D*, close fitting division board, by which the capacity of the hive is regulated. The honey board on which the surplus receptacles rest is composed of strips of board one-fourth inch thick, secured in a manner to prevent sagging and by which all the surplus honey may be at once removed. The receptacles consist of six boxes, each of which is composed of four section frames, holding two pounds each. The frames are close fitting at sides and top, and are bound firmly together by strips of tough manilla paper which are glued across the sides and turned around the end one-fourth inch to hold the glass in place; *A*, represents a strip of this paper ; *B*, one section of the box. We thus have all the advantages of large boxes for storing and handling, combined with all the advantages of neat two pound sections which may or may not be glassed, but our advice is to use no glass except in the crate.

We have given the illustration and discription of our Eclective Hive at the request of a very large number of subscribers, and will here state that of all we have sent out we have not had one word of fault from purchasers, but on the other hand we have received numerous high commendations.

1 Hive, complete in all respects..$5 00
5 to 20 Hives, complete in all respects, each...................................... 4 00
Materials complete, except nails and glass, in lots of 5 or more, each....... 2 50

BELLOWS SMOKER.

By our last improvement in the Bellows Smoker we believe we have rendered it superior to any and all others now before the public. It is made of the very best material; has the direct draft to perfection; burns all kinds of combustibles; utilizes all the wind and smoke; never goes out while there is burning material in the fire barrel, and invariably gives unbounded satisfaction, It is also an indispensible article in the greenhouse and where ever destructive insects congregate. Also old combs may be so thoroughly fumigated with it as to destroy all eggs or larvæ of the moth miller.

The size of our New Smoker is the same as Bingham's standard, which is plenty large enough for all purposes.

PRICE, $1.00. By Mail, $1.25.

GLOVES.

Long Rubber Gloves (manufactured for us) by mail, per pair................$ 2 00
Per dozen, by express.. 18 00

Always send the size you want by laying the open hand, palm down, on a piece of paper and mark around it with pencil.

ALL METAL GEARED HONEY EXTRACTORS,
CHEAP AND DURABLE.

By the use of the Honey Extractor the apiarian is enabled to control the amount of honey in the hive and keep the bees and queen at work in the breeding apartment, when they would not enter and work in the surplus boxes, Often in the midst of a good honey harvest the hives become so crowded with honey as to leave no empty cells in which the queen may deposit eggs to keep up the strength of the stock, and the workers having no more space to fill in the body of the hive, hang idly around, and often collect in large bunches at the entrance of the hives.

Muth's All Metal Extractor (see cut), complete with knife.................$12 00
Improved Root Extractor, suitable for any frame not more than 14x20 inches, with fine spring steel bent shank knife, honey gate all complete..$8 50 to $10.00
Honey Knives... 1 00

    The points of superiority of the Muth over the Improved Root or "All Metal" are as follows: First. It is deeper and will hold several gallons below the revolving basket. Second, The shape of the basket keeps the honey frame in its place and also prevents throwing honey over the top. Third, The upright crank Fourth, The covers. etc

    We will promptly furnish either machine on receipt of price, or if no knife is needed $1.00 may be deducted.

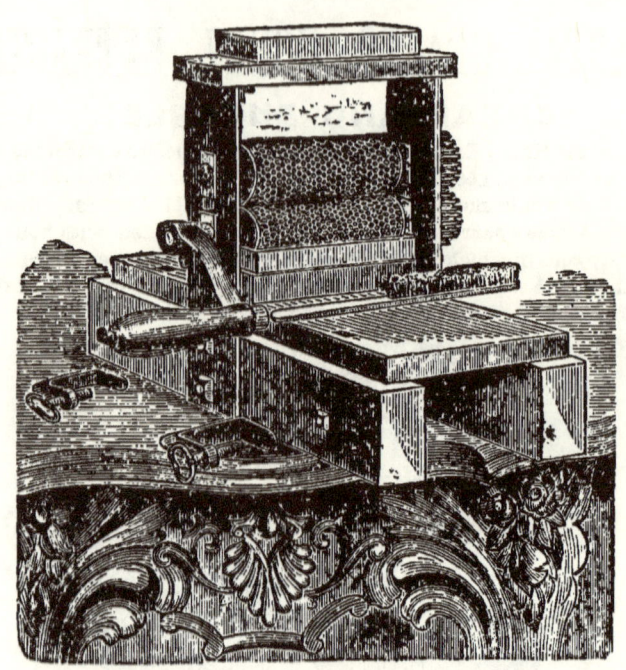

COMB-FOUNDATIONS

Have now been extensively, and thoroughly tested by all the prominent apiarists of America, and the uniform verdict is that it is a grand success, and of equal value with movable frames, in the line of *profitable bee-keeping*.

PURE *yellow* BEES-WAX is the *only material fit to be used in its manufacture*. We are prepared to promptly fill all orders at the following prices:
One to ten lbs. 55 cents per lb. Fifty pounds or over, 50 cents per lb. One hundred pounds or more, 45 cents per lb.

We make no extra charge for packing. Our largest sheets are 12x24 inches, and run from 5 to 8 square feet to the pound Our packing boxes are thin and light, and paper is placed between the sheets In ordering, give inside dimensions of frames. Purchasers pay express or freight charges, but if ordered by mail add twenty-five cents per pound to above prices for postage and extra packing. Samples by mail, post paid, five cents.

ITALIAN BEES AND QUEENS.

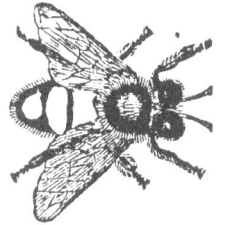 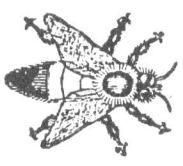 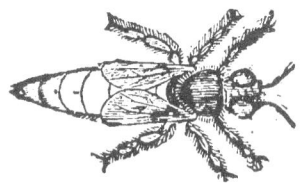

We shall, as heretofore, supply our customers with only CHOICE STOCK, as we know, by experience, that a poor article, especially of *live stock*, is *dear* at any price, while a *good* article is CHEAP at a fair price.

The following are as low as *we can afford* to sell, consistent with a very moderate profit:

Full stocks of pure Italian Bees, in movable frame hives, each,	$15 00
Three frame nucleus stocks in American or Eclectic hive, with tested queen	9 50
Imported Queens from best districts in Italy	6 00
Home bred Italian queens, *guaranteed* to be bred from and fertilized by as good a strain of the genuine Italian as can be found in the world, sent in May	4 00
In June, each	3 50
Same sent from July to October	2 50
" " " " " by the half dozen, at one time, each	2 00
Italian Queens ordered from other breeders, safe arrival *only* guaranteed, each	1 00
Cyprian Queens bred direct from imported mothers and *fertilized by Cyprian Drones*, each,	5 00
Two for $8.00, or three for $10.50. Full stocks in new frame hives	20 00

Safe arrival in all cases guaranteed.

BEE VEILS.

Black Bobinet with elastic cord by mail	$ 50
Per dozen, by mail	4 80

BEES-WAX EXTRACTOR.

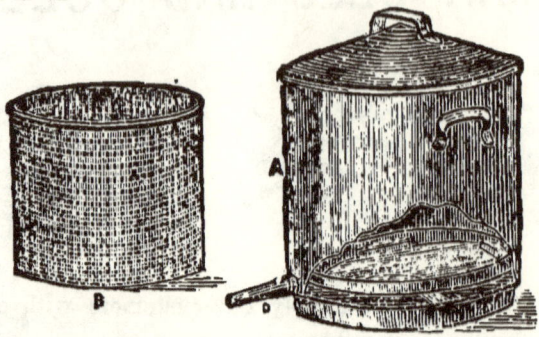

By the use of this machine all the old black useless comb and scraps are turned into nice yellow bees wax, by steam process.

Sent by express..$3 50
Hot water attachment, extra... 75

SEEDS OF HONEY PLANTS.

Lucerne Clover Seed by mail post paid, ℔ 1 lb...................$ 60
White   "   "   "   "   "   60
Melilot   "   "   "   "   "   60
Alsike   "   "   "   "   60
Rape Seed....   "   "   "   30
Chinese Mustard Seed "   "   "   60
Rocky Mountain beeplant, by mail, per 2 oz package.............. 20
Borage Seed..........   "   "   "   50
Mignonette..........   per lb.........................1 50
Catnip................   "   " 2 00
Silver Hull Buckwheat (half pound).............................. 30

For these and all other seeds in large quantities write us for wholesale prices.

OUR BEE FEEDER.

Some of its advantages over other feeders are the following: *Much or little* may be fed without any *change* in the feeder. When refilling the bees or heat cannot escape. You can always see just how fast the bees are consuming the food without touching the feeder. As it allows no heat to escape from the hive, it may be used at all seasons of the year with perfect safety. It will feed thick or thin syrup as the case may be.

Our new Bee Feeder, by mail.....................................$ 75
Sent by express, per doz.. 6 00

All money sent by postoffice orders, drafts *on New York city banks,* or, lastly, in *registered* letters, are at our risk. Address,

ORANGE JUDD COMPANY,

Or,   *245 Broadway,* NEW YORK,

A. J. KING & CO., 61 Hudson St., New York.

www.ingramcontent.com/pod-product-compliance
Lightning Source LLC
Chambersburg PA
CBHW021809230426
43669CB00008B/683